PRINCIPLES OF BANKING & INSURANCE

FOR B.B.A. (3RD SEMESTER) OF BHAGAT PHOOL
SINGH WOMEN'S UNIVERSITY, KHANPUR

ANNU SEHRAWAT

THE CONSTITUTION OF INDIA

PREAMBLE

WE, THE PEOPLE OF INDIA, having solemnly

resolved to constitute INDIA into a SOVEREIGN

SOCIALIST SECULAR DEMOCRATIC REPUBLIC

and to secure to all its citizens:

JUSTICE , social , economic and political ;

LIBERTY of thoughts , expression , belief faith and worship ;

EQUALITY of status and of opportunity ;

and to promote among them all ;

FRATERNITY assuring the dignity of the individual

and the unity and integrity of the nation ;

WE DO HEREBY GIVE TO OURSELVES THIS CONSTITUTION.

Contents

Foreword   *vii*

Preface   *ix*

Prologue   *xi*

1. Insurance Concept   1

2. Irda Act - 1999   18

3. Life Insurance   27

Important Terms About Life Insurance Policy

4. Life Insurance Public And Private Sector   65

   Companies In India

5. Life Insurance Act- 1956   91

6. General Insurance   100

7. General Insurance Companies   108

8. Bank Concept   118

9. Concept Of Bank Management   140

10. Legal Framework Of Regulation Of Bank   157

Foreword

BPS University, KHABPUR has revised the course contents of BBA course. This book has been especially written for the new syllabus of paper code : BBL 211 **"Principles of Banking and Insurance".** Some of the distinguishing features of the book are as follows :

- Full coverage of the prescribed syllabus.
- Systematic and sequential arrangement of topics as per the syllabus.
- Lucid and simple language.

I am sure that this book would be very useful both students and teachers. Suggestions and critical comments for improvement of the book are welcome.

Author : **Annu Sehrawat**
Studies at BBA 2nd year
Website : annusehrawat8520.blogspot.com
E- Mail : annusehrawat8520@gmail.com
Management Department
GCW GOHANA

Preface

I would like to express my special thanks of gratitude to my Teacher **"Dr. Prashant Kumar, Babita Mor & Mr. Kapil"** as well as our Principal **"Mr. Dinesh Singh "** who gave me the golden opportunity to do this wonderful work "write a book" , which also helped me in doing a lot of Research and i came to know about so many new things. I am really thankful to them.

Secondly, I would also like to thank my **PARENTS** and friends who helped me.

Author : Annu Sehrawat

Studies at Bachelor of Business Administration (2nd year)

Prologue

SYLLABUS

BPS UNIVERSITY, KHANPUR

BBA (3rd Semester)

PRINCIPLES of BANKING AND INSURANCE

Paper Code : BBL - 211

UNIT- 1

Inusrance - Concep, Nature, Classification - Life & Non-Life, Functions, Importances and Principles of Insurance; IRDA Act 1999 - Organization, Guidelines for life and Non- Life Insurance.

UNIT - 2

Life Insurance - Concept; Public & Pvt. Sector Companies in India- Their Products, Schemes & Plans ; LIC Act 1956- An Overview.

UNIT- 3

General Insurance- Concept, Types; Public & Pvt. Sector Companies in India- Their Products, Schemes and Plans.

UNIT- 4

Bank- Concept, Classification their Objective & Funtions. Bank Management- Concept, Functions, Importance. Legal Framework of Regulation of Banks : Banking Regulations Act 1949 and Main Amendments, RBI Act 1934 and main amendments. Banking Forms- Corporate Banking, Rural Banking, Retail Banking, International Banking, E-Banking. Banker- Customer relationships: payment and collections of cheques; Special services rendered by banks to customers. Reforms in Banking after 1991.

CHAPTER ONE

Insurance concept

Insurance is a means of protection from financial loss. It is a form of risk management, primarily used to hedge against the risk of a contingent or uncertain loss.

An entity which provides insurance is known as an insurer, an insurance company, an insurance carrier or an underwriter. A person or entity who buys insurance is known as a policyholder, while a person or entity covered under the policy is called an insured. Policyholder and insured are often used as but are not necessarily synonyms, as coverage can sometimes extend to additional insureds who did not buy the insurance. The insurance transaction involves the policyholder assuming a guaranteed, known, and relatively small loss in the form of payment to the insurer in exchange for the insurer's promise to compensate the insured in the event of a covered loss. The loss may or may not be financial, but it must be reducible to financial terms, and usually involves something in which the insured has an insurable interest established by ownership, possession, or pre-existing relationship.

The insured receives a contract, called the insurance policy, which details the conditions and circumstances under which the insurer will compensate the insured, or their designated beneficiary or assignee. The amount of money charged by the insurer to the policyholder for the coverage set forth in the insurance policy is called the premium. If the insured experiences a loss which is potentially covered by the insurance policy, the insured submits a claim to the insurer for processing by a claims adjuster. A mandatory out-of-pocket expense required by an insurance policy before an insurer will pay a claim is called a deductible (or if required by a health insurance policy, a copayment). The insurer may hedge its own risk by taking out reinsurance, whereby another insurance company agrees to carry some of the risks, especially if the primary insurer deems the risk too large for it to carry.

Nature of insurance

1. CONTRACT:

The most important feature of insurance is that it is legal contract between the insurer and insured, under this insurer promises to compensate the insured for the loss which is mentioned in the policy and the insured promise to pay a fixed rate of premium which is consideration in this contract for the promise of the insurer. It is a type of contract where one party agrees to compensate in case of loss suffered by another party.

2. UNDERTAKING OF RISK:

In insurance contract, bearing and protecting of risk is the subject matter of the contract. For example paying of insured amount in case of death of the assured, loss by fire or happening of marine perils. The risk is undertaken by the insurer to compensate the insured on the happening of the risk mentioned in the policy. The insurance company bears the risk and make good the loss. It restores the person standing as it was before the loss, it provides a mental relief to the insured that in case of loss, the insured will undertake his risk.

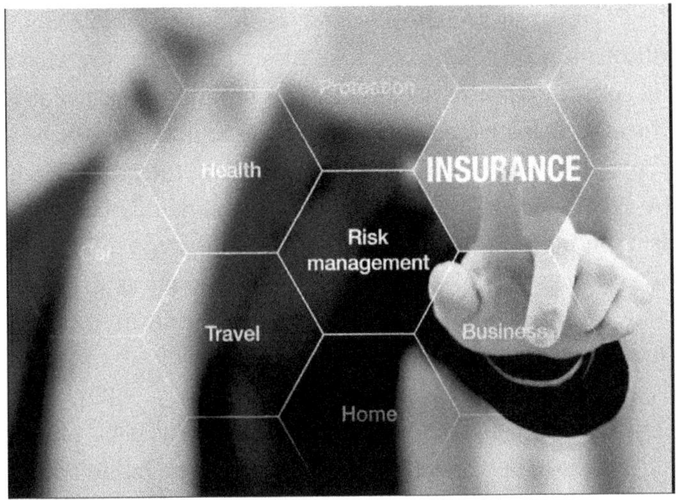

3. A COOPERATIVE DEVICE:

Insurance is cooperative device of sharing the burden of risk

of one on the shoulders of many. All the insured contribute the premium out of which the person who actually suffers loss is compensated or is paid up, insurance is a device to share the financial loss of few among many others.

4. PAYMENT OF POLICY AMOUNT ON THE HAPPENING OF EVENTS:

On the happening of a specified event, the insurance company is bound to make good the loss to the insured. Happening of an event is specific in life insurance that is death, but it is not so in case of marine, fire or accidental insurance. In life insurance, a fixed amount is paid but in indemnity insurance (fire, marine, etc) amount of payment is uncertain depending upon the quantum of damage.

5. PREMIUM:

Payment of premium by the insured is another feature of an insurance contract. Like other contracts, the factor of consideration is fulfilled by the premium because it is the subject for which insurer promises to undertake or bear the risk if insured. In absence of premium, the promise will be NUDAM PACTUM, hence void. To conclude insurance is a method to transfer the risks from insureds to insurers who agrees to it for a consideration known as premium and promises to bear and compensate the insured on the specified extent of loss.

6. CONTRACT OF ADHESION:

It means it is contract which is not arrived by mutual negotiations between the parties, It means he has to adhere to the policy in which way it is offered there is no chance if bargain. It means the insured accepting the policy must accept whole of it he cannot accept one part of and leave the another. All he can do is that he can select the most appropriate policy among various policies which the insurer is offering.

7. DEVELOPMENT OF LARGER INDUSTRIES:

Insurance helps industries to develop who have more risk in their setting up, the owner may get the industries assets insured and in case of loss he will be compensated. The financial institution may be ready to give credit to such industrial units which have insured their assets including plant and machinery etc.

8. PROVIDE PROTECTION:

Insurance provides protection against future risk, accidents, uncertainty. It protects the insured against all the losses which are specified or for which the insurance is done.

CONCLUSION:

The above-mentioned feature makes us clear that insurance is a contract between two parties and it is a cooperative device to undertakes the loss, it protects the insured against the loss by the insurer in return of premium paid by the insured. Thus, it is clear that insurance makes good the loss.

Classification life & Non life insurance:-

1. Life Insurance

Just like the name suggests, life insurance is a cover for your life. Life insurance can offer your family monetary relief in difficult times. This type of insurance provides financial security to the nominee (spouse, children, etc.), in case of an unfortunate event. It also serves as an investment tool in some cases.

2. General Insurance

While life insurance covers the life of a person, general insurance provides cover to other aspects and assets in a person's life, for example, health, car, travel, home, etc. This type of cover insures assets against theft or damage due to fires, natural calamities, accidents, man-made disasters like riots or terrorist attacks, etc. While life insurance policies provide cover against the risk of life, general insurance provides cover against other types of risks that may affect a person's health or some of his/her physical assets like a home or a vehicle etc.

Key differences between General and Life Insurance

- **Term of contract :-** One major distinction between the two is the duration of the policy. Life insurance plans are long term plans and require policyholders to either pay a lump sum premium, or regular monthly, quarterly, or yearly premiums for a significant amount of time. For example, 15-20 years or up to a lifetime. General insurance, on the other hand, is a short term plan that is generally renewed yearly.
- **Premium payment :-** The premium for a life insurance policy is paid at regular intervals like monthly, quarterly, or yearly. In contract, the premium for a general insurance policy is paid at once, either when the policy is bought or when it is renewed. This may differ in case of a travel insurance plan, where a person pays premium only while buying insurance for a specific trip.
- **Insurance Claim :-** In case of a life insurance policy, the sum assured is paid to the nominee during the policy term in the event of the policyholder's death. The sum assured can also be returned to the policyholder on maturity. In the case of endowment and money back plans, the insurance provider also pays back the interest earned on investments. Another important thing to note is that in case of a critical illness, the policyholder can claim life insurance benefits upon diagnosis of the disease or health condition covered under the policy, if the relevant rider is chosen during the purchase of the policy. The insurance claim of a general insurance can depend on some specific events. For example, general health insurance can only be claimed after

hospitalisation, in case of a medical emergency or ailment diagnosis, depending on the policy. In the same manner home, motor, or travel insurance can be claimed only if there has been any loss or damage to an asset due to an unfavourable event like a robbery, accident, or any such event.

- **Policy Value** :- The policy value for a life insurance plan depends on the preference of the policyholder. One can fix the sum assured depending on the requirements of his/her family and the ability to pay premiums. The sum assured is then paid back to the policyholder on maturity or to the nominee in case of an unfortunate event. As opposed to life insurance, the policy value of general insurance is influenced by the value of the asset. The policy value, in this case, is based on the damage suffered and not on the sum assured.

Functions of Insurance

Functions of insurance are to spread the loss caused by a particular risk over several persons, who are exposed to it and who agree to insure themselves against the risk. The most important function of insurance is to spread the risk over a number of persons who are insured against the risk, share the loss of each member of the society on the basis of the probability of loss to their risk and provide security against losses to the insured. So, insurance functions are;

- The system to spread the risk over several persons who are insured against the risk;
- The principle to share the loss of each member of the society based on the probability of loss to their risk; and

- The method to provide security against losses to the insured.

The functions of insurance can be studied into two parts;

- **Primary Functions, and,**
- **Secondary Functions.**

Primary Functions of Insurance

1. Insurance provides certainty

Insurance provides certainty of payment at the uncertainty of loss. The uncertainty of loss can be reduced by better planning and administration. But, the insurance relieves the person from such a difficult task. Moreover, if the subject matters are not adequate, the self-provision may prove costlier. There are different types of uncertainty in a risk. The risk will occur or not, when will occur, how much loss will be there? In other words, there is the uncertainty of happening of time and amount of loss. Insurance removes all these uncertainties and the assured is given certainty of payment of loss. The insurer charges the premium for providing the said certainty.

2. Insurance provides protection

The main function of insurance is to protect the probable chances of loss. The time and amount of loss are uncertain and at the happening of risk, the person will suffer the loss in the absence of insurance. The insurance guarantees the payment of loss and thus protects the assured from sufferings. The insurance cannot check the happening of risk but can provide for losses at the happening of the risk.

3. Risk-Sharing

The risk is uncertain, and therefore, the loss arising from the risk is also uncertain. When risk takes place, the loss is shared by all the persons who are exposed to the risk. The risk-sharing in ancient times was done only at the time of damage or death; but today, based on the probability of risk, (he share is obtained from every insured in the shape of premium without which protection is not guaranteed by the insurer.

Secondary Functions of Insurance

Besides the above primary functions, the insurance works for the following functions:

4. Prevention of loss

The insurance joins hands with those institutions which ate engaged in preventing the losses of the society because the reduction in loss causes the lesser payment to the assured arid so more saving is possible which will assist in reducing the premium. Lesser premium invites more business and more business causes lesser share to the assured. So again premium is reduced to which will stimulate more business and more protection to the masses. Therefore, the insurance assists financially to the health organization, fire brigade, educational institutions and other organizations which are engaged in preventing the losses of the masses from death or damage.

5. It Provides Capital

The insurance provides capital to society. The accumulated funds are invested in the productive channel. The death of the capital of the society is minimized to a greater extent with the help of investment in insurance.

The industry, the business, and the individual are benefited by the investment and loans of the insurers.

6. It Improves Efficiency

Insurance eliminates worries and miseries of losses at death and destruction of property. The carefree person can devote his body and soul together for better achievement, it improves not only his efficiency but the efficiencies of the masses are also advanced.

7. It helps Economic Progress

The insurance by protecting the society from huge losses of damage, destruction, and death, provides an initiative to work hard for the betterment of the masses. The next factor of economic progress, the capital, is also immensely provided by the masses. The property, the valuable assets, the man, the machine and the society cannot lose much at the disaster.

<u>importance of insurance</u>

Insurance has evolved as a process of safeguarding the interest of people from loss and uncertainty. It may be described as a social device to reduce or eliminate risk of loss to life and property. Insurance contributes a lot to the general economic growth of the society by provides stability to the functioning of process. The insurance industries develop financial institutions and reduce uncertainties by improving financial resources.

1. Provide safety and security:

Insurance provide financial support and reduce uncertainties in business and human life. It provides safety and security against particular event. There is always a fear of sudden loss. Insurance provides a cover against any sudden loss. For example, in case of life insurance financial assistance is provided to the family of the insured on his death. In case of other insurance security is provided against the loss due to fire, marine, accidents etc.

2. Generates financial resources:

Insurance generate funds by collecting premium. These funds are invested in government securities and stock. These funds are gainfully employed in industrial development of a country for generating more funds and utilised for the economic development of the country. Employment opportunities are increased by big investments leading to capital formation.

3. Life insurance encourages savings:

Insurance does not only protect against risks and uncertainties, but also provides an investment channel too. Life insurance enables systematic savings due to payment of regular premium. Life insurance provides a mode of investment. It develops a habit of saving money by paying premium. The insured get the lump sum amount at the maturity of the contract. Thus life insurance encourages savings.

4. Promotes economic growth:

Insurance generates significant impact on the economy by mobilizing domestic savings. Insurance turn accumulated capital into productive investments. Insurance enables to mitigate loss, financial stability and promotes trade and commerce activities those results into economic growth and development. Thus, insurance plays a crucial role in sustainable growth of an economy.

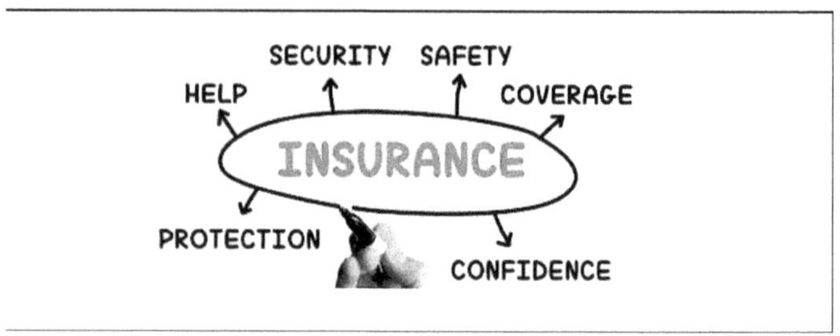

5. Medical support:

A medical insurance considered essential in managing risk in health. Anyone can be a victim of critical illness unexpectedly. And rising medical expense is of great concern. Medical Insurance is one of the insurance policies that cater for different type of health risks. The insured gets a medical support in case of medical insurance policy.

6. Spreading of risk:

Insurance facilitates spreading of risk from the insured to the insurer. The basic principle of insurance is to spread risk among a large number of people. A large number of persons get insurance policies and pay premium to the insurer. Whenever a loss occurs, it is compensated out of funds of the insurer.

7. Source of collecting funds:

Large funds are collected by the way of premium. These funds are utilised in the industrial development of a country, which accelerates the economic growth. Employment opportunities are increased by such big investments. Thus, insurance has become an important source of capital formation.

<u>Principles of insurance</u>

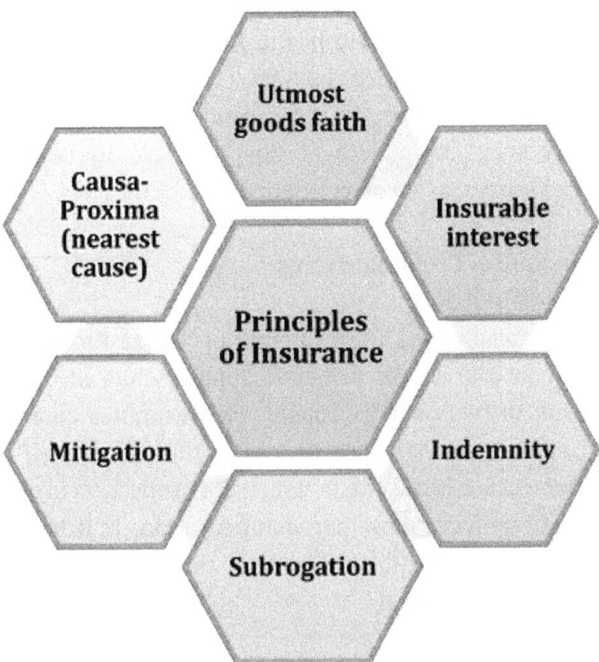

Principles of Insurance

The concept of insurance is risk distribution among a group of people. Hence, cooperation becomes the basic principle of insurance.

- **Principle of Utmost Good Faith**

The fundamental principle is that both the parties in an insurance contract should act in good faith towards each other, i.e. they must provide clear and concise information related to the terms and conditions of the contract. The Insured should provide all the information related to the subject matter, and the insurer must give precise details regarding the contract.

Example – Jacob took a health insurance policy. At the time of taking insurance, he was a smoker and failed to disclose this fact. Later, he got cancer. In such a situation, the Insurance company will not be liable to bear the financial burden as Jacob concealed important facts.

- **Principle of Proximate Cause**

This is also called the principle of 'Causa Proxima' or the nearest cause. This principle applies when the loss is the result of two or more causes. The insurance company will find the nearest cause of loss to the property. If the proximate cause is the one in which the property is insured, then the company must pay compensation. If it is not a cause the property is insured against, then no payment will be made by the insured.

Example – Due to fire, a wall of a building was damaged, and the municipal authority ordered it to be demolished. While demolition the adjoining building was damaged. The owner of the adjoining building claimed the loss under the fire policy. The court held that fire is the nearest cause of loss to the adjoining building, and the claim is payable as the falling of the wall is an inevitable result of the fire. In the same example, the wall of the building damaged due to fire, fell down due to storm before it could be repaired and damaged an adjoining building. The owner of the adjoining building claimed the loss under the fire policy. In this case, the fire was a remote cause, and the storm was the proximate cause; hence the claim is not payable under the fire policy.

- **Principle of Insurable interest**

This principle says that the individual (insured) must have an insurable interest in the subject matter. Insurable interest means that the subject matter for which the individual enters the insurance contract must provide some financial gain to the insured and also lead to a financial loss if there is any damage, destruction or loss.

Example – the owner of a vegetable cart has an insurable interest in the cart because he is earning money from it. However, if he sells the cart, he will no longer have an insurable interest in it. To claim the amount of insurance, the insured must be the owner of the subject matter both at the time of entering the contract and at the time of the accident.

- **Principle of Indemnity**

This principle says that insurance is done only for the coverage of the loss; hence insured should not make any profit from the insurance contract. In other words, the insured should be compensated the amount equal to the actual loss and not the amount exceeding the loss. The purpose of the indemnity principle is to set back the insured at the same financial position as he was before the loss occurred. Principle of indemnity is observed strictly for property insurance and not applicable for the life insurance contract.

Example – The owner of a commercial building enters an insurance contract to recover the costs for any loss or damage in future. If the building sustains structural damages from fire, then the insurer will indemnify the owner for the costs to repair the building by way of reimbursing the owner for the exact amount spent on repair or by reconstructing the damaged areas using its own authorized contractors.

- **Principle of Subrogation**

Subrogation means one party stands in for another. As per this principle, after the insured, i.e. the individual has been compensated for the incurred loss to him on the subject matter that was insured, the rights of the ownership of that property goes to the insurer, i.e. the company. Subrogation gives the right to the insurance company to claim the amount of loss from the third-party responsible for the same.

Example – If Mr A gets injured in a road accident, due to reckless driving of a third party, the company with which Mr A took the accidental insurance will compensate the loss occurred to Mr A and will also sue the third party to recover the money paid as claim.

- **Principle of Contribution**

Contribution principle applies when the insured takes more than one insurance policy for the same subject matter. It states the same thing as in the principle of indemnity, i.e. the insured cannot make a profit by claiming the loss of one subject matter from different policies or companies.

Example – A property worth Rs. 5 Lakhs is insured with Company A for Rs. 3 lakhs and with company B for Rs.1 lakhs. The owner in case of damage to the property for

3 lakhs can claim the full amount from Company A but then he cannot claim any amount from Company B. Now, Company A can claim the proportional amount reimbursed value from Company B.

- **Principle of Loss Minimisation**

This principle says that as an owner, it is obligatory on the part of the insurer to take necessary steps to minimise the loss to the insured property. The principle does not allow the owner to be irresponsible or negligent just because the subject matter is insured.

Example – If a fire breaks out in your factory, you should take reasonable steps to put out the fire. You cannot just stand back and allow the fire to burn down the factory because you know that the insurance company will compensate for it.

CHAPTER TWO

IRDA Act - 1999

IRDA Act 1999 – Organization

Insurance Regulatory and Development Authority of India (IRDA). IRDA stands for insurance Regulatory and Development Authority of India. It is an autonomous and the statutory body tasked with regulating and promoting insurance and reinsurance in the country. IRDA was constituted by the Insurance Regulatory and Development Authority Act - IRDA Act, 1999 and has its headquarters in Hyderabad, Telangana. In the recent times, IRDA has moved on to a more digital platform to help and cater the needs of both the Insurance companies, agents and policyholders. Every year IRDA online exam is conducted and the exam results are displayed on the IRDA website.

Brief History of Insurance

in India Insurance in India dates back to the 19th Century with the establishment of Oriental Life Insurance Company in Kolkata in 1818. The Indian Life Insurance Assurance Companies Act of 1912 was the first law that regulated life insurance in the country. Life Insurance Corporation was established in the year 1956 with the nationalisation of the life insurance sector. The LIC absorbed then currently functioning 154 Indian and 16 non Indian insurers and 75 provident societies.

LIC enjoyed a complete monopoly till the late 1990s when the insurance sector was opened to the private sector general insurance in India, on the other hand, began during the Industrial Revolution with the establishment of Triton Insurance Company in Kolkata in 1850. In the year 1907, the Indian Mercantile Insurance was formed. It was the first company to underwrite all the classes of general insurance. In 1957, a wing of Insurance Association of India – General Insurance Council – was established to frame the code of conduct and regulate the means of fair business practices.

The General Insurance Business (Nationalisation) Act was passed in 1972 and the insurance industry was nationalised on January 1st 1973. A hundred and seven insurers were amalgamated and formed a group of four insurance companies – National Insurance Company, New India Assurance Company, Oriental Insurance Company and United India Insurance Company. The General Insurance Corporation of India (GIC Re) was established in 1971 and was effective on January 1st 1973. By the year 1991, the Government of India began to plan the economic reforms in the insurance sector. For the purpose, a committee was formed in 1993 for the reforms in the insurance sector. The committee was headed by Shri R. N. Malhotra (Retired Governor of the Reserve Bank of India). The Malhotra Committee recommended some major reforms in the insurance sector such as allowing private sector companies to promote insurance in the country, allowing foreign promoters in the domestic insurance market and formation of an independent regulatory body answerable to Parliament and the Government. An interim body called Insurance Regulatory Authority was set up in 1996. In the year 1999 Insurance Regulatory and Development Authority (IRDA) Act was passed and on April 19th 2000, Insurance Regulatory and Development Authority (IRDA) of India received autonomous status.

Structure of IRDA

IRDA is a ten-member body that consists of: One Chairman (for five years and maximum age of 60 years) Five whole-time members (for five years and maximum age of 62 years) Four part-time members (not more than five years) The chairman and the members of IRDA are appointed by the Government of India. Current Chairman of IRDA is Mr Subhash Chandra Khuntia.

Objectives of IRDA

To promote the interests and rights of the policyholders. To promote and monitor the growth of the insurance industry. To prevent frauds and misselling of insurance product and ensure speedy settlement of genuine claims To bring transparency and proper code of conduct in financial markets dealing with insurance.

Functions and Duties of IRDA:

According to Section 14 of IRDA Act of 1999, the agency has the following functions and duties:.

- Issuing the registration certificates to insurance companies and regulate them
- Protect the interests of the policyholders
- Provide licences to insurance intermediaries like agents and brokers after stating the required qualifications and set guidelines for their code of conduct
- Promote and regulate professional organisations related to insurance to enhance the development of the sector
- Regulate and supervise the premium rates and terms of the insurance policies
- Specify the conditions and manners by which the insurance companies have to present their financial reports

- Regulate the investment of the policyholders' funds by the insurance companies.
- Ensure the maintenance of the solvency margin i.e. the ability of an insurance company to pay out claims.. Read more at: https://www.fincash.com/l/insurance/irda

Guidelines for life and non life insurance:-

Introduction:

Insurance agents play a key role in conservation of insurance business by rendering valuable post sale service to policyholders. Whenever an agent discontinues his agency or is terminated by the Insurance Company, the policies secured by the agent are left behind orphaned. In order to fill the gap created by the exit of insurance agents in servicing the insurance policies as also to promote the persistency of insurance policies, the Authority issues the following guidelines under Section 14 (2) (e) of Insurance Regulatory and Development Authority Act, 1999.

Guidelines on Servicing of Orphan Policies

Definitions:

1. '*Orphan life insurance* policies'for the purpose of these Guidelines, means the policies initially effected by an individual insurance agent whose services were subsequently terminated or removed or deleted from the rolls of the insurer excluding those policies to which the

effecting agent is entitled to renewal commission under provisions of Section 44 of the Insurance Act. The policies that are considered eligible under section 40(2A) of Insurance Act also do not fall under the purview of this definition.

2. *"Allottee Agent"* for the purpose of these guidelines is an individual insurance agent who has completed atleast 2 years of service as an insurance agent and on the rolls of the life insurance company to whom the orphan, lapsed life insurance policies are allotted for the purpose of conservation and rendering policy services.

3.*'A lapsed life insurance policy'* for the purpose of these guidelines is a policy on which premium remains unpaid even after six months from the due date

Guidelines:

4. *Insurance companies* are allowed to allot any of the lapsed orphan life insurance policies to individual insurance agents whose license is in force for the purpose of conservation and rendering effective policy service to the policyholders. Only an orphan life insurance policy that is in lapsed condition on the date of allotment is eligible for allotment.

5. Single Premium Life Insurance policies or life insurance policies on which no further premiums are due for payment (Limited Premium Payment Policies after the expiry of Premium Paying Term) are not eligible for allotment under these guidelines. Life Insurance Products designed with specific marketing features, inter alia, say direct / online marketing where no commission outgo is projected under respective File and Use are also not eligible for allotment.

6. The Life Insurers shall notify the particulars of *'Allottee Agent'* to the concerned policy holders.

7. The 'Allottee agent' shall be provided with a list of such allotted life insurance policies along with the addresses for policy servicing. While submitting the list, it shall be stipulated that the purpose of submitting the said list is for rendering required policy services including revival and any details thereof shall neither be parted with to any third party / entity nor be used for any other business purposes. However there is no bar in an 'Allottee agent' canvassing new policies to the policyholder after reviving the lapsed allotted policies.

a. As a prudent measure, in the event of surrender of an allotted policy after allotment, but before revival / reinstatement, no new business shall be accepted by Life Insurer from the same allottee agent on the life of the same policyholder until the expiry of 6 months from the date of surrender of the orphan lapsed life policy.

8. It shall be specified to the 'Allottee agent' that the objective of the allotment is the conservation/revival and further servicing of the policies.

9. Regulation 8 of IRDA (Licensing of Individual Agents) Regulations, 2000 (Code of Conduct) applies to the 'Allottee agent' in respect of all the allotted policies. It shall be disclosed upfront to the 'Allottee agent'.

10. While allotting the policies for servicing, the life insurers shall direct the Allottee agents that all policy services shall be rendered similar to how an insurance agent would do to those policies that were otherwise effected by him / her.

11. The insurers are allowed to pay the following remuneration to the 'Allottee agent' towards policy service in respect of the policies allotted to him/her.

a. Equivalent to the commission rates mentioned in the respective File & Use.

b. The remuneration referred to in 11 (a) above is payable only on revival of a lapsed orphan policy on account of arrears premiums received on or after the date of allotment and also on subsequent renewal premiums paid under the policy.

c. No upfront / advance payments to agents are allowed on account of the policy allotments referred herein.

d. The payment of remuneration shall cease with the exit of an 'Allottee agent' by any means and such 'Allottee agent' will not be eligible for the benefits accorded by Section 44 of the Insurance Act.

12. The policies that are allotted for servicing shall not be counted for persistency of the *allottee agent*.

13. The allotment of lapsed policies shall be done judiciously by the life insurers keeping in view the ability / feasibility of the insurance agents to service the policies allotted subject to the following condition.

a. The number of policies allotted to an agent shall not exceed 20% of the total number of policies that were introduced by him/her and in force as on the date of allotment.

14. Insurers shall also take into account the track record of the agent and complaints registered against an agent etc. while allotting the orphan policies.

15. Insurers shall have in place a Board approved policy for allotment of lapsed orphan policies which is in compliance with these guidelines.

16. The Life Insurers shall take an undertaking from the agents regarding their willingness for the proposed allotment and their consent for rendering the required policy services.

17. Where the lapsed orphan policy allotted is not revived / reinstated within 6 months from the date of such allotment, life insurers shall have the discretion to undo the allotment by issuing a formal notice to the 'Allottee agent' and re-allot to any other agent as per the norms prescribed herein.

18. An allotted policy which was revived or reinstated but lapsed subsequently may also be allotted in accordance with the provisions of the within referred stipulations, despite the *allottee agent* being an active agent on the rolls of the Life Insurer.

19. Allotting the lapsed orphan policies by a life insurance company is only an option.

20. The Insurers shall put in place procedures for capturing the details of allotment of lapsed orphan policies and the Allottee agents who are servicing the allotted policies, in order to ensure that the objectives of allotment are met.

21. All Life Insurers shall put in place measures in accordance to Point no. 2 and. 2 (b) of IRDA Circular No. 31/IRDA/CA/CIR/Sep-09 dated 02.09.2009 to service all lapsed orphan policies that do not fall within the definition of these guidelines.

22. All Life Insurers shall submit the periodical reports relating to allotments referred in these guidelines in the specified format, if any, as and when called for by the Authority.

23. These Guidelines will come in to force with immediate effect.

life insurance

Concept of life insurance :-

The gift of life is precious, and you cannot put a money tag on it. But one needs money for survival and to satisfy the needs of the family. If there is a sudden demise of the breadwinner, the family might face difficulties. Hence, to ensure the proper livelihood of the family even after the death of bread earner, it is often advised to buy a life insurance policy.

What is a life insurance policy?

Wondering about the meaning of life insurance? A life insurance policy is essentially a contract between an individual and an insurance provider, where the company promises to pay a specified amount of money to the family or beneficiary of the individual, in return for regular payments over a period of time. These payments are known as premium and are usually paid on an annual basis. The individual who buys the insurance is known as the policy holder.

Life insurance assures lump sum amount to be paid to the family if the policyholder passes away unexpectedly. Though money cannot make up the loss, it ensures no financial hiccups to the family even after the demise of the breadwinner.

The life insurance policy provides with the much-needed cover against risk and offers you opportunities to grow your savings It is also an effective tool that enables you to save for future expenses that may occur, such as the higher education or marriage of children.

Life insurance has meaning especially for those with minor children, children with special needs, those who wish to secure the financial future of their family or wish to build savings over the long term.

It is best to buy a policy early, since the premium amount rises with age and if the individual is a smoker or has pre-existing medical conditions.

Benefits of life insurance

Here are some of the benefits of life insurance:-

• **Tax benefits:–** Enrolling for a life insurance policy can guarantee you tax benefits. The premiums you pay towards the policy make you eligible for tax exemptions of up to ?1.5 lakhs of your taxable income, under Section 80C of the Income Tax Act. The death benefits are also fully tax exempt, under Section 10(10)D of the ITA.

• **Guarantee of fix returns:-** Life insurance policies guarantee that you get a fixed amount after a fixed timeline. You need to go through the structure of different life insurance products. Read through the structure and terms and conditions of different life insurance products to choose a policy that best suits your needs. Whatever you choose, you can rest assured that the promised death benefits will be disbursed to the beneficiary, if the information provided by you at the time of enrolling for the policy was accurate.

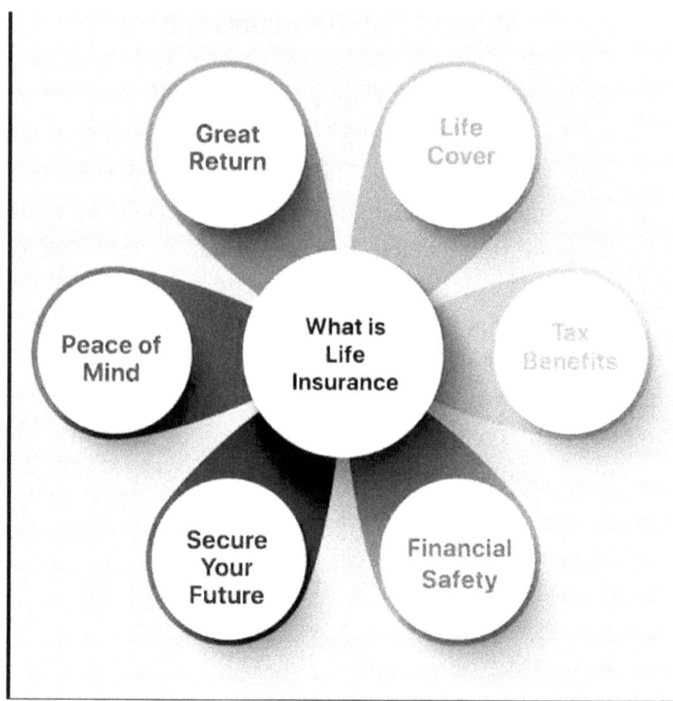

• **Risk mitigation and coverage:-** These policies provide the quintessential risk coverage in terms of monetary compensations to mitigate and cover risks after the policyholder's death. By enrolling for life insurance, you are protecting your family against financial risks that would occur if the primary breadwinner meets an untimely death.

• **Provision for loan:-** Certain policies provide the option of loan and allow to borrow a sum of money. This means that if you need to take on a loan, for instance, to fund the education or marriage of a child, you can use the life insurance policy as collateral.

• **Health expense coverage:-** Most of these policies cover the health and treatment expense that may occur. occur if the policy holder falls ill. You can also choose riders to increase the coverage of the insurance policy to protect your finances even while you are alive.

- **Financial Protection for Family :-** A life insurance policy will provide a specified sum to your family (the chosen nominee) at the time of your untimely demise. They can use the sum assured to fulfil various financial needs.
- **Critical Illness Benefit :-** You can opt for <u>critical illness</u> rider with a life insurance policy, which offer protection against critical health ailments, such as cancer, kidney failures, and cardiovascular issues. This way, you or your family need not worry about the financial side of medical emergencies
- **Peace of Mind:-** With the best life insurance policy by your side, you get peace of mind, knowing that there is a financial safety net your loved ones can bank upon after you.
- **Extensive Coverage at Low Cost:-** insurance companies offer significant payouts for <u>life insurance</u> (like term plan) at a low premium, depending on your age and health condition.
- **Opportunities to Create Wealth:-** Life insurance plans like ULIP (Unit Linked Insurance Plan) gives you the benefit of life cover along with market linked returns from your investment.

- **Financial Planning for Life:-** Along with providing financial support against the event of untimely demise, life insurance plans also work as long-term investments to meet various goals in life. By investing in life insurance at the right age, you can plan well for different life stages.

- **Planning for your Child's Higher Education:**- Saving money for your child's education might be one of the biggest priorities for you, being an Indian parent. By investing in the best life insurance policies, you can plan for your child's future and help him secure various educational milestones in life.

- **Assured Income for Retirement:**- Life insurance is a financial instrument that you can choose to plan for retirement. The steady payouts it can offer in the form of annuities can become the source of income for your retired life.

- **Redemption of Mortgage:** Life insurance policies serve as the best possible tool for the coverage of loans and mortgages availed by the policyholder. If there is ever any unforeseen situation due to which the policyholder is not able to repay his / her loan or mortgage, the bereaved family members will not have the burden of repayment, and the policy can be used to repay the loan or mortgage.

- **Loan Facility:** Individuals who avail life insurance policies will have the choice of availing a loan against their insurance policy, which could help them meet their unplanned life stage requirements without hampering the benefits provided by the policy they have purchased.

- **Growth via Dividends:** Conventional life insurance policies provide customers with an opportunity to take part in the economic growth while taking no investment risk whatsoever. While the policyholder split the investment income through yearly announcements of bonus / dividends, the policyholder will earn maturity benefits in addition to contributing to economic growth

- **Guaranteed Income via Annuities:** When it comes to planning for retirement, there are few instruments as effective as life insurance policies. Since you will be saving money over a period of time, life insurance policies will help in providing a steady source of income after you have retired from professional life.

- **Profitable and Secure Long**-Term Investment: The insurance industry is highly regulated. The Insurance Regulatory and Development Authority of India has implemented several regulations through which the money of the policyholder is ensured to be safe with the stakeholders, which means that all the money you invest in your life insurance policy will be the responsibility of the stakeholders of the company through which you avail your policy. Since life insurance is a long-term savings product, it also ensures that the policyholder focuses on long-term returns rather than focussing on risky investment decisions that could provide short-term profits.

- **Promotes Savings in the Long Run:** Since life insurance policies are long-term agreements wherein the policyholder is required to make a fixed periodical payment, it helps the policyholder inculcate the habit of savings. Saving money regularly over a relatively long period of time helps in building a good corpus which will in turn help in meeting your financial requirements at different stages of life.

- **Comprehensive Plan for Different Stages of Life:** Not only does life insurance offer financial support in case of the policyholder's unforeseen and accidental death, but also serves as a long-term investment in the sense that it encourages you to lay down your objectives, whether it is the education of your children, their marriage, constructing the home of your dreams, or even planning for a peaceful retired life. The planning will be done based on your risk appetite and life stage. Most conventional life insurance plans, such as traditional endowment plans, provide specific maturity benefits and built-in guarantees via a number of product options like Guaranteed Maturity Values, Guaranteed Cash Values, Money Back, etc.

types of life insurance policies

Following are the different types of life insurance policies available today in the market:-

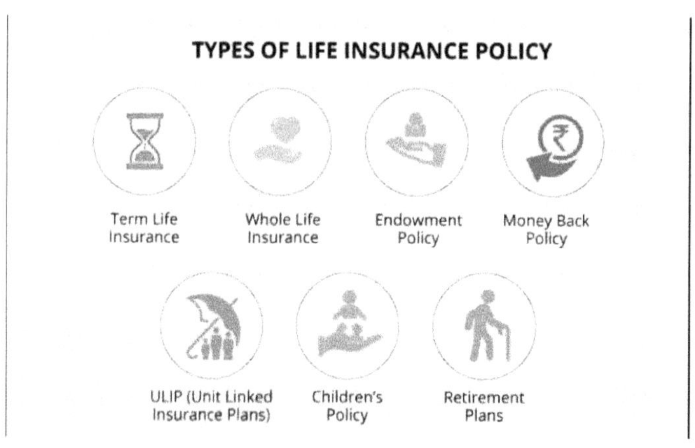

• **Term Life Insurance**

Term insurance policies provide the predefined amount of money to the policyholder's family, only if the policyholder dies during a specified term. No claim if the insured person survives till the end of the policy period. This policy essentially remains active for a predefined time and is one of the affordable policies available in the market.

• **Whole life insurance**

Whole life insurance as the name suggests provides you cover at all points of your life in which the policy is in force. This coverage time can go as long as 100 years. These policies also offer loan facilities to the policyholder. The overall process of buying is simple and can be done online as well through a simple process.

• **Money Back Policy**

The main difference and advantage of money back policy is that it gives the policyholder different survival benefits which are linked to the period of the policy. Unlike other policies, this policy gives you money during the policy period. Regardless of the instalments paid, if the policyholder dies, the family gets the entire sum. These policies are expensive as compared to other counterparts.

• **Endowment Policy**

Endowment policies are different from term insurance policies in a way that in case of these policies, the insured gets a lump sum amount of money if s/he survives till the maturity date. The policy offers insurance with savings at the same time. They also come with riders that may be used to increase the coverage of the policy. In case of death, the endowment policy guarantees that along with the sum a participation profit is also paid according to the nature of the policy.

• **Retirement Plans**

Retirement plans, in simple terms, can be defined as those plans that guarantee fixed income after your retirement. They aid in creating a retirement corpus. This corpus is then invested to generate post-retirement money flow, thus creating a financial cushion and helping in risk mitigation. The money is rolled out in the form of monthly pension. All in all, these policies help the insurer in achieving the financial goals of long term nature.

In the advent of the internet, almost all the companies claim to have the best life insurance online. However, one must read the fine print carefully and should check carefully, if the policy offerings match with individual requirements.

- **ULIP Plans**

ULIPs provide the flexibility of premium payment. You have the option to move your money between equity and debt funds. ULIPs allow you to withdraw a part of your money whenever you need it. You can also choose where to invest, depending on your risk appetite.

Principles of Life Insurance

In India, we follow four basic principles of life insurance.

1.Insurable Interest: This principle has been put in place to protect insurance policies against any kind of misuse. It refers to the level of interest that the potential policy holder is estimated to have in the life insurance policy. This interest could be in the form of a personal relationship, family bond, etc. Based on this interest level, the insurance company approves or rejects the individual's application for a policy.

2. Minimal Risk: Any company that provides life insurance is taking on some level of risk, since they would need to pay the assured sum at some point of time. Therefore, the company would prefer to keep the level of risk as low as possible. To ensure this, the insurer might check the applicant's medical status, smoking habits, etc. In addition, they might expect the policy holder to take good care of their health.

3.Good Faith: As mentioned earlier, a life insurance policy is essentially a contract between the insurer and the policy holder. This contract is entered into on good faith that both parties are providing accurate relevant information, without hiding anything. If any information is withheld, it could lead to serious consequences. For instance, if the insurance provider discovers that the policy holder had a pre-existing heart condition but did not divulge the fact at the time of policy purchase, they could reject the claim made by the beneficiary, following the demise of the policy holder.

4.Law of Large Numbers: This is a key principle of life insurance, which is based on a statistical theorem that states that with larger numbers, fluctuations tend to average out. This essentially means that since life insurance is a long-term investment, the losses and gains will average out over time, minimizing the risks for the policy holder.

Important Terms About Life Insurance Policy

1. What is a Policy?

Policy means the contract of insurance entered into between you and the insurance company as evidenced by this document, the Proposal Form, the Schedule and any additional information/document(s) provided to the insurance company, in respect of the Proposal Form along with any written instructions from you subject to the insurance company's acceptance of the same and any endorsement issued by the insurers.

2. What is Sum Assured?

It refers to the amount payable to a nominee after the event of the unfortunate demise of the insured, as specified in the chosen life insurance policy. You can use an online life insurance premium calculator to get an estimate of the premium payable for a specific sum assured.

3. What is Annualised Premium?

Annualised Premium is the essentially the amount specified in the Policy Schedule, and denoted the Premium payable during a Policy Year chosen by you (as policyholder), excluding any additional premium paid for the Underwriting, loadings for modal premium, Rider Premiums and applicable taxes, cess, or levies, if any;

4. What is Life Insurance Coverage Period?

It is the duration for which the insured is covered under a life insurance policy. It can be different from the premium payment term/period during which you need to pay a life insurance premium.

5. What is Maturity Date for the life Insurance Policy?

It is the means the date specified in the Schedule, on which the Policy Term expires;

6. What is Life Insurance Premium?

It denoted an amount specified in the Policy Schedule, payable by You, by the due dates to secure the benefits under the Policy, excluding applicable taxes, cess, and levies, if any.

7. What is Premium Payment Mode or Frequency?

An individual can pay the life insurance premium in:

1. Regular mode, which is monthly, quarterly, half-yearly, or annually throughout the policy tenure

2. A specific premium payment tenure, which can be a certain pre-fixed number of years (not till the end of the policy term)

8. What are Life Insurance Riders?

Riders are essentially features, which are in addition to basic benefits under the Policy. These include accidental death benefit rider, critical illness rider, and waiver of premium rider.

Q. How to Select the Best Life Insurance Policy?

With a multitude of life insurance plans available in the market, it is critical to choose the right one. The selection of a life insurance plan must be based on a broad spectrum of financial needs.

Here are a few steps to consider while buying the best life insurance policy:

1. Gain Knowledge About Various Types of Life Insurance

Without proper knowledge of how life insurance works, people feel incapacitated to decide about buying the right policy. Hence, it is crucial to gain a thorough understanding of different types of life insurance products before zeroing in on any of them.

2. Assess Your Financial Needs

A life insurance plan that is suitable for your peers may not be ideal for you. Thus, you must consider your specific needs, be it affordability, choice of sum assured or riders before you start comparing different plans.

3. Compare Plans in Terms of Benefits

Owing to the wide variety of life insurance plans available, you need to be sure you select the right one which offers adequate benefits. For this, you should do the required homework of comparing the plans across several parameters like premium, the sum assured, and investment component, if any.

Q. How to Choose the Best Life Insurance Company for Your Family?

The selection of the right life insurance provider is essential to ensure that you or your loved ones will get the benefits they seek from the purchase plan.

Consider the following aspects while choosing the best life insurance provider:

1. Claim Settlement Ratio (CSR)

This ratio defines the claims settled by an insurer over the ones received in a financial year. The higher the CSR, the higher are the chances of getting your life insurance claim paid.

2. Solvency Ratio

It refers to how well an insurance company can manage sufficient cash flow to deal with the debts. An insurer can provide hassle-free claim settlement if this ratio depicts its strength to meet the related liabilities.

3. Premium

All life insurance plans are priced differently. Thus, you need to choose the one that seems cost-effective for you. To avoid the risk of losing the life cover, make sure you do not select a plan whose premium is too high and unaffordable to you.

4. Persistency Ratio

It defines the percentage of policyholders that pay the premium over the total active policyholders. It is a good indicator of customer satisfaction delivered by the insurer.

5. Claim Settlement Process

A simplified claim settlement procedure implies your family will not have to face any hassle to receive life insurance benefits. It is advisable to choose an insurance company which follows a streamlined process to settle claims.

Q. Documents Required to Get Life Insurance Plan

You need the following officially valid documents [3][5][6] while purchasing life insurance from a renowned insurer:

- Passport
- Voter ID
- NREGA job card
- Aadhar Card
- PAN Card/Form 60

In case these documents do not contain the updated address, you need the following documents:

- Utility bills of any service provider
- Property tax receipt
- Family Pension Payment Orders issued to the retired individuals
- Letter of allotment of accommodation from the employers such as PSUs and other statutory bodies

Q. How Do You Save Tax with Life Insurance Plan?

Being insured in today's date is of utmost importance. Even if your partner has a life insurance policy and a group policy from his/her company, it is important that you purchase a comprehensive life cover for yourself. Covering your life will not reduce the emotional distress that you may be going through, but a life insurance policy will ensure that you have adequate financial backup during times of your need. The insurance market is currently flooded with insurers selling a horde of insurance products and services. While selecting a particular life insurance policy, it is imperative to understand the tax implications of the same.

- **Section 80C of the Income Tax Act Deduction:** If you are currently paying a premium towards your life insurance policy or for the life of your parents, children, or spouse, you will be eligible for a deduction under Section 80C of the Income Tax Act. Irrespective of whether your child is a minor or not, the deduction shall be applicable. However, in order to be able to claim the said deduction, the premium amount (being paid by policyholder) must not be more than 10% of the sum assured amount, in case the policy was issued after 1 April 2012.
- **Section 10(10D) Maturity Deduction:** If the premium amount (being paid by policyholder) does not surpass 10% of the sum assured for plans that have been issued post 1 April 2012 and 20% of the sum assured for plans that have been issued before 1 April 2012, then the maturity amount that the policyholder receives at the end of the policy term will be completely exempt from tax as per Section 10(10D) of the Income Tax Act, 1961.

Q. How Can You Pay for Life Insurance Policy?

You can choose to pay the premium of life insurance plans in one go or with regular payments over time. Life insurance policies usually provide the option to choose between a single (one time) payment, regular (throughout the policy tenure) payment and limited premium payment tenure (for a payment tenure less than the policy coverage period).

With regular premium payment mode, you can select any of the following payment options:

- **Annual**
- **Semi-annual**
- **Quarterly**
- **Monthly**

You must also know that the life insurance premiums paid online are processed through secure payment gateways, thus ensuring the safety of transactions.

Q. How Will Your Family Receive the Life Insurance Claim Money?

After your (Life insured) untimely demise, your loved ones will get the policy benefits by claiming the same from your insurer.

Follow these steps to claim life insurance policy benefits:

1. Inform the insurer at the earliest

2. Ask for the claim intimation form

3. Ask for the documents to be submitted with the claim form

4. If the policy was bought online, apply for the claim online as well

The nominee of a policy should not wait too long after the insured's demise to ensure quick and easy claim settlement.

Q. What is the Right Life Insurance Cover for You?

Once you have decided to buy life insurance, the next big step is to choose a specific life cover, or sum assured. Here are some aspects to keep in mind while determining a ballpark figure for the life cover:

1. Consider Your Working Years

A life insurance plan serves as an income replacement tool. Hence, you need to consider the number of active working years it would replace while choosing the sum assured. For instance, if you are 25 right now and have planned your retirement at the age of 50, you have 25 future earning years to consider.

2. Chart Out Your Regular Expenses

The sum assured should cover recurring financial outgoes, including household expenses, bills, and existing loan EMIs on a year-on-year basis. By charting out these expenses for a specific period, you will get a better idea of the sum assured to be chosen.

3.Consider Landmark Stages in Your Family's Life

Certain stages or events in life require large lump sum amounts. These include wedding, retirement, or child's higher education. The sum assured should cover them all majorly to ensure your family will not face a financial burden after you.

Q. How does life insurance Policy work?

A life insurance policy provides a sum assured to the nominee in case of the untimely demise of the life insured individual. There are different types of life insurance plans that you can choose based on your goals and protection needs.

Q. Why should I buy life insurance Policy?

With life insurance, you can make sure that the financial security of your loved ones in your absence, is never compromised. The insurance benefits they receive will help them finance their regular expenses and life goals.

Q. How to Claim Life Insurance?

Life insurance claims are made under two circumstances:

- Death of the life insured
- Maturity of the life insurance policy

Q. Life insurance Claims in Case of Death:

Here, nominees or close relatives of the deceased makes the claim (or assignees if the policy has been assigned) in the following way:

- Inform the insurer as soon as possible with details such as time of death, place of death and cause of death.
- Submit certain documents and proofs to the insurer. This will include:

- The death certificate of the deceased person along with the claim form as provided by the company.
- The policy in its original form as this is a legal document and proof of an insurance agreement that covered the life of the deceased.
- Discharge form which has to be signed with witnesses.
- If the policy was assigned, the assignee will have to provide the deed.
- If a claim is made by someone other than the nominee or assignee, the person making the claim will have to submit legal proof of his/her title.
- If required, post-mortem reports and hospital and attending doctor's reports will also have to be submitted.
- In cases involving police inquiries, an inquest report will have to be submitted.

While these outline the standard set of documents required to process a claim, other evidence may be required such as an employer's certificate or any other forms or reports that will help resolve any issues thrown up during an insurer's claim verification or investigative processes.

Q. Rules for Beneficiaries Claiming Life Insurance:

When a policyholder's beneficiary or nominee is claiming life insurance, he or she will be required to follow certain simple rules. The nominee will have to file a death claim in order to procure the death benefit. If you have a physical insurance policy, you can take a claim intimation or a notification form from your life insurance provider. If you have an online policy, you can apply for a form online.

- Your claim intimation will need to comprise elements such as policy number, name of the policyholder, place of death, name of the insured, name of the claimant, etc.
- The nominee will first have to fill a few death claim forms and also provide some proof of death. Once the form is filed with the life insurance company, then it is established that the company has got a death claim.
- Next, the nominee will need to assemble all the appropriate documents that serve as proofs.
- Then, the nominee will need to furnish these documents to the company for the claim settlement process.

- Once the forms and documents are submitted, the company will verify everything and then make a decision if the claim should be settled or not.

Q. Factors Affecting Life Insurance Policy Premiums:

- If an individual is overweight or obese, he/she will be required to pay extra premiums for his/her life insurance policy.
- If an individual is part of a risky occupation like race car driving, insurance companies are typically skeptical towards such professions because of their high risk. Hence the premiums are high.
- If an individual is a smoker, his/her risks are increased, and hence, he/she will be required to pay extra premiums towards the life insurance policy.
- If an individual is a heavy drinker, he/she will be required to pay extra premiums.

Q. Which is better, term life or whole life insurance?

Term life plans are offer a high sum assured at low premium rates. Such plans do not offer any returns and are valid for a limited period of time. Whole life plans, on the other hand, offer death benefits as well as savings benefits. Unlike term plans, these plans are valid for the entirety of the policyholder's life.

Both types of policies have their own perks. You must assess your needs first to decide which is better. If you seek high coverage at low premium rates, then term plans are a better option. However, if you want life cover as well as savings benefit with a longer tenure, a whole life plan will be a perfect pick.

Q. At what age should you buy life insurance?

Life insurance prices are heavily influenced by your age. As you grow older, the premium rates will increase as old age makes us more vulnerable to risks. Ideally, you should invest in a life insurance plan in your late 20s or early 30s. The ideal age varies based on the number of dependents you have. If you have a history of any critical illness in your family, it is advisable to invest in a plan as soon as possible.

Q. Can I get life insurance at 62?

Yes, you can buy life insurance at 62 years. Most life insurance policies have a maximum entry age ranging between 55 years and 60 years. However, there are numerous policies that are designed specifically for senior citizens. Such plans are useful for individuals who haven't invested in a plan earlier in life. Certain plans for senior citizens also offer retirement benefits and pay outs.

Q. What happens to life insurance if you don't die?

Life insurance policies are designed in a way to provide your family/nominee with financial support after your demise. The death benefit can be availed only if the policyholder dies within the policy period. But, in case you survive the policy period, the death benefit won't be paid out.

For traditional plans and policies with benefits, if you survive the policy term, you will receive the maturity benefit. But in the case of term plans, the policy ceases to exist after you survive the term.

Q. What is not covered by life insurance?

The exclusions under life insurance plans may differ from one policy to another. However, there are certain exclusions that almost all policies agree with. Mentioned below are some important ones:

- Death caused while performing criminal or unlawful activities
- Death caused by man-made disasters like war, riot, etc.
- Suicide or any self-inflicted injury
- Death caused while participating in adventure sports or any dangerous activities like bungee jumping, rock climbing, etc.
- Death from HIV or any other sexually transmitted diseases
- Death or harm caused by indulging in illegal intoxicants
- Death caused during the waiting period is not covered by life insurance policies

Q. Do I need life insurance if I am single?

Life insurance is an important investment if you have a family or dependents. Usually, people who are single do not require a life cover but that is not the only factor which you must consider. Whether single or married, if you have loved ones depending on your income, you must buy a life insurance policy as after your demise, the burden of expenses will fall on your loved ones.

Q. What deaths does life insurance cover?

Death under the following conditions are covered under life insurance plans:

- Death due to medical conditions
- Natural death
- Accident related death

How long do you pay for whole life insurance?

The premium payment term for whole life insurance plans can be any of the following:

- **Level premium**: In this case you will pay a specific premium till you are alive. For instance, if you are paying Rs.3,000 as a premium, the same rate will continue throughout the tenure without any changes.
- **Limited payment**: In this plan, you will be required to pay the premium for a stipulated amount of time. The premium payment term can be 10 year, 20 years, etc. The premium rates in such plans are usually high.
- **Single premium**: You will be required to pay a lump sum premium at the start of the policy in single premium plans.

- **Intermediate premium**: Such plans have two premium rates. Initially a lower premium rate is charged, after which the insurer assesses the interest, actual mortality and other similar factors to establish a new rate that has to be paid for the rest of the policy term.

Q. How do I choose the best life insurance policy?

Choosing a life insurance policy depends on your financial protection needs. Ideally, life insurance should be opted for to provide financial protection to your dependents in the unfortunate event of death. Term insurance policies are considered the best form of pure protection as they offer the highest coverage for the lowest premiums. These plans offer only death benefits. To receive maturity or survival benefits as well as death benefits, you will have to opt for TROP policies, endowment policies, pension or annuity policies, money back policies or ULIP policies.

Q. Why do term insurance policies offer higher life coverage than other types of insurance policies?

Premiums paid by a term insurance policyholder are fully utilised towards creating a life cover. Under other types of life insurance plans, only a part of the premium paid is allocated towards creating a life cover. The balance is utilised to provide for maturity benefits or as in the case of ULIPs a part of the premium is used to meet administration and sales expenses. This makes term insurance plans more affordable than other plans. This is why they are also called pure protection plans because they only offer a pay-out in the event of death of the life assured. Other plans offer returns as well as life coverage.

Q. How do I choose the sum assured and tenure of my life insurance policy?

In general, it is recommended that a person avails a cover that is at least 20 times his/her current income. However, this depends on your personal financial situation and personal profile. If you have to provide for many dependents, you would need a larger cover. If you are young, you should opt for a longer term life cover to take advantage of lower premiums. As you grow older, premiums rise for the same sum assured. Again, if you don't have other savings avenues, a large sum assured will serve the purpose better. Always, remember to account for inflation as well. Consider loan obligations or debt that will have to be serviced in your absence. Many people ensure the chosen sum assured will cover debts in their absence. Another pertinent factor is affordable. Higher the sum assured, higher the premiums.

Q. Do life insurance policies cover only death or accidents and illnesses as well?

Life insurance policies are meant to provide financial sustenance in the event of death, primarily. However, most policies offer additional coverage for disability, accident and various illnesses. These are called riders and usually come at an additional cost although some policies do offer them as part of the primary plan.

Q. Is it safe to buy life insurance online?

Yes, these days almost all insurance providers offer online purchase of life insurance. Additionally, a number of financial services providers offer this option through their websites, where you can compare and choose from a number of providers. The fact that people are increasingly turning to online purchases of life insurance policies signifies how secure the process is. Online purchases offer policyholders of comfort and convenience and in many cases the policies are cheaper since there are no sales agents involved.

Q. Can premiums be paid in instalments or are they payable in a lump sum?

Depending on the type of policy chosen, premiums can be paid either in a lump sum or in regular instalments.

Q. What is the difference between a reversionary bonus and terminal bonus?

Bonuses are offered under participating life policies i.e. policyholders can participate in the profits of the policyholder's fund. A reversionary bonus is declared as a percentage which applies to the chosen sum assured. Reversionary bonuses can be simple or compounded bonuses. One-off reversionary bonuses are those that are paid out of one-time profits that may not occur again. A terminal bonus is the residual bonus declared on maturity or the policy i.e. if after declaration of all reversionary bonuses, there are still profits accrued to the fund, it may be paid out to the policyholder in the form of a terminal bonus.

Q. What is a policy's 'free-look period'?

As per IRDA regulations, if a policyholder does not wish to continue his/her policy they can discontinue the same within the first 15 days of buying it and get a refund.

Q. What is the 'surrender value' of a policy?

If a policyholder wishes to cancel his/her policy, once in effect, they can surrender it to the insurer and receive the surrender value as a refund. The surrender value is calculated based on premiums paid and how long the policy was in effect. Surrender is usually allowed after a certain period of time.

Q. What is meant by 'assignment' of a policy?

If, for example, a policy is used to raise a loan, the policy is 'assigned' or transferred to the lender. The policy then bears the lender or the 'assignee's' name. Once the loan is repaid the policy can be reassigned or transferred back.

Q. What must I consider before purchasing a life insurance policy?

When purchasing a life insurance policy, the most important thing to check is whether or not guaranteed returns will be provided by the plan. You must also keep an eye on the lock-in period, information regarding premium payments, the implications of defaulting on premium payments, the revival conditions, the fees that would be charged for cancelling or surrendering the policy, the availability of a loan facility, etc. Go through the terms and conditions of the policy you wish to purchase and make sure that it meets all your requirements for an affordable cost.

Q. How important are proposals and all the disclosures that are made in them?

Proposals are key components on insurance and policies are underwritten based on the disclosures made in them. It is essential that you provide only correct disclosures and statements to the insurance company or you will be at risk of rejection of claims.

Q. What medical reports will I have to submit to avail a life insurance policy?

Insurance companies may request medical reports from applicants depending upon the age at which they purchase the insurance policy, their age when the policy matures, personal and family history, sum assured, and other factors they consider crucial. For instance, if the applicant is obese, special reports such as Glucose Tolerance test or Electro Cardiograms could be requested. Similarly, depending upon your medical condition, the insurance company may ask you for one or more reports.

Q. How do life insurance companies calculate the surrender value of an insurance policy?

The surrender value of a policy is usually a percentage of the policy's paid-up value. Insurance companies calculate the surrender value of an insurance policy based on the surrender value factor, which is the ratio between the premiums paid and the period for which premium payments have not been made.

Q. What are the formalities involved when submitting a maturity claim?

Almost all insurance companies send an intimation along with the discharge voucher to you at least two to three months before the date of maturity. The intimation will inform you as to how much money you will be receiving from the insurance provider. The discharge voucher as well as the policy bond must be duly signed by the policyholder and returned to the insurance provider as soon as possible as the sooner you do so, the sooner will they be able to release your payment. In case you have assigned the policy to another individual, only the assignee will be authorised to receive the claim amount at the time of maturity.

Q. What are settlement options?

At the time of purchasing a life insurance policy, the insurance provider may design and define the manner in which you will receive the payout. Settlement options are offered by most insurance companies and they ensure that you receive your money in a manner that was specified when you were purchasing the insurance policy.

Q. What are the documents that my nominees must furnish in case I die during the policy term?

In case of your unfortunate and untimely demise during the policy term, your nominees will have to furnish such basic documents as the policy bond, the claim form, and the death certificate of the late policyholder. There may be instances wherein the insurance company may also request you to furnish other documents like a post mortem report, a police inquest report, an employer's certificate, a hospital certificate, a medical attendant's certificate, etc. The policy bond usually contains all the information associated with the claims process.

Q. What are the major differences between a non-participating policy and a participating one?

A non-participating insurance policy is one that does not allow the insured individual to share in the profits made by the company, while a participating policy ensures that an insured individual has the right to share in the profits of the company. However, the dividends or bonuses declared by the insurance company may increase or decline based on the life funds' investments returns.

Q. What does the company do in case I do not make premium payments on time?

Insurance companies provide something called a grace period to customers who are unable to make premium payments on the due date. The period usually spans for 15 to 30 days, and customers who default on their premium payments are expected to pay during this period. Failure to do so will mean that your life insurance policy has lapsed. As a result, you can either reinstate or revive the policy within a predetermined period of time.

What happens if my policy is cancelled during the free-look period?

Cancellation of policies during the free-look period can be done free of cost. However, in case you wish to cancel your life insurance policy after the free-look period, you will be charged a small fee for the same.

Q.What is the payout granted to an individual who surrenders his / her life insurance policy?

When a life insurance plan has been active for a specified number of years (usually at least five), the policy acquires a cash value. Every life insurance policy has a savings portion called the cash value. The cash value of a life insurance policy adds up when the worth of premium payments made by the policyholder exceeds the cost of insurance. This excess amount is transferred to a cash value account where it accrues interest. In case you choose to surrender the policy, the company will offer you the cash value or surrender value of the policy. However, please note that surrendering an insurance policy prior to the end of the maturity period will make you incur a significant loss.

CHAPTER FOUR

Life Insurance Public and Private Sector Companies in India

At the end of March 2018, there are 24 life insurance companies operating in India, including a

public sector company named Life Insurance Corporation of India and remaining 23 private sector companies competing with LIC for Life Insurance Business in India. All private and public sector life

insurance companies in India were selected for the study. The companies selected for the research work are as follows.

(a)Public Sector:

Life Insurance Corporation of India.

(b)Private Sector:

1.AEGON Life Insurance Co. Ltd.
2.Aviva Life Insurance Co. India. Ltd.
3.Bajaj Allianz Life Insurance Co. Ltd.

4.Bharti Axa Life Insurance Co. Ltd.

5. Birla Sun Life Insurance Co. Ltd.

6.Canara HSBC Oriental Bank of Commerce Life Insurance Co. Ltd.

7.DHFL Pramerica Life Insurance Co. Ltd.

8.Edelweiss Tokio Life Insurance Co. Ltd.

9.Exide Life Insurance Co. Ltd.

10.Future Generali India Life Insurance Co. Ltd.

11.HDFC Standard Life Insurance Co. Ltd.

12.ICICI Prudential Life Insurance Co. Ltd.

13.IDBI Federal Life Insurance Co. Ltd.

14.India First Life Insurance Co. Ltd.

15.Kotak Mahindra Old Mutual Life Insurance Ltd.

16.Max Life Insurance Co. Ltd.

17.PNB Met Life India Insurance Co. Ltd.

18.Reliance Nippon Life Insurance Co. Ltd.

19.Sahara India Life Insurance Co. Ltd.

20.SBI Life Insurance Co.Ltd.

21.Shriram Life Insurance Co.Ltd.

22.Star Union Dai-ichi Life Insurance Co.Ltd.

23.Tata AIA Life Insurance Co. Ltd.

16.Max Life Insurance Co. Ltd.

17.PNB Met Life India Insurance Co. Ltd.

18.Reliance Nippon Life Insurance Co. Ltd.

19.Sahara India Life Insurance Co. Ltd.

20.SBI Life Insurance Co.Ltd.

21.Shriram Life Insurance Co.Ltd.

22.Star Union Dai-ichi Life Insurance Co.Ltd.

23.Tata AIA Life Insurance Co. Ltd.

16.Max Life Insurance Co. Ltd.

17.PNB Met Life India Insurance Co. Ltd.

18.Reliance Nippon Life Insurance Co. Ltd.

19.Sahara India Life Insurance Co. Ltd.

20.SBI Life Insurance Co.Ltd.
21.Shriram Life Insurance Co.Ltd.
22.Star Union Dai-ichi Life Insurance Co.Ltd.
23.Tata AIA Life Insurance Co. Ltd.

Life Insurance Companies Brief Details

Aditya Birla Sun Life Insurance Company

Aditya Birla Sun Life Insurance came in to existence with the joint venture between Aditya Birla Group and Sun Life Financial Inc. The company is known as a pioneer of Unit Linked Life Insurance plans and has over 600 branches spread over 500 cities across the country. A complete range of insurance services is offered by Aditya Birla Sun Life Insurance like protection plan, child plan, health and retirement solution, ULIP plan, customized group product and life stage product to provide complete satisfaction to the customers.

Aegon Life Insurance Company

AEGON Life Insurance is focused to provide a customer centric business along with an excellent and innovative working professionals. Started its operation in year 2008 the company works with a multiple channel distribution strategy with an aim to help people to plan their life in a much better way. The company has launched an array of products that focuses on offering plans to the customers to meet their financial goal. The plans offered by the company are term plan, endowment plan, Group plan, ULIP plan, pension plan, protection plan, saving plan, child plan and ruler plan

Ageas Federal Life Insurance Company

Formed in 2008 Ageas Federal Life Insurance is a joint venture between Ageas Bank, Federal Bank and Ageas a European Insurance Company. With a partnered network of 2137 branches over the country the company offers a wide range of capital management solution, protection and retirement to the corporate customers as well as individual. The bank also offers ingenious technological solution to its customers. To be eligible for Ageas Federal Life Insurance one should have a minimum age limit of 18 years to maximum age limit of 55 years.

Aviva Life Insurance Company

Aviva Life Insurance company is a joint venture between the Dabur Group and Aviva Group. With 121 networked centers across the country Aviva Life Insurance serves a large number of customer base countries wise. Among the other insurance companies in India the company is known to first introduce Unit Link and Unitized With-Profit Plan in the market. The Aviva Life Insurance Company offers a wide variety of plans to the customers. These plans fulfill all the needs and necessities of the buyers at a very economical price. Some of the most common plans offered by the company are protection plan, ruler plan, child plan, retirement plan, saving plan, health plan, term plan and group insurance plan.

Life insurance companies

Bajaj Allianz Life Insurance Company

Bajaj Allianz Life Insurance is a joint venture between the European financial services company Allianz SE and Bajaj Finserv Limited. Among the other life insurance companies in India Bajaj Allianz Life Insurance Company meet its customers need by providing them a huge range of products right from ULIP and Child Plan to Group and Health Insurance. The company provides a huge array of customized products that cater the every single demand of the customer and provide them a transparent benefit. Launched in year 2001 this life insurance company provides a one stop solution to the customers and help them in achieving their financial goals.

Bharti AXA Life Insurance Company

Headquartered in Mumbai Bharti AXA Life Insurance is a life and general insurance provider company. The company is a joint venture between Bharti Enterprises and AXA Group. The customers can choose from the wide range of policies offered by the company ranging from investment plans to traditional plan or life insurance plan to child plan. The company is flourishing immensely and has a network of 123 offices in different cities across India. The customers has witnessed a maximum grievances resolved by the company in a year and had experienced a claim settlement ratio of 97.28%. The policies offered by the company have a maximum tenure of 65 years and the age criteria for the plans starts from minimum 18 years to maximum 65 years.

Canara HSBC OBC Life Insurance Company

Launched on year 2008 Canara HSBC OBC Life Insurance is a joint venture between HSBC Insurance Holding Ltd, Canara Bank and Oriental Bank. The company works as a pan India network with around 7000 branches of the three shareholder banks across the country. Moreover, the company provides necessary training and coaching to the bank staff across the 28 centers in country. With a huge customer base the company provides most customized products to meet the needs of the buyers. The policies offered by the company have a maximum tenure of 40 years and the eligibility criteria range from minimum 18 years – maximum 70 years.

Edelweiss Tokio Life Insurance Company

Edelweiss Tokio Life Insurance established in 2011 is a newly formed private sector insurance provider in India. Edelweiss Group of India and Tokyo Marine Holding of Japan joined hand together and has formed Edelweiss Tokio Life Insurance Company. The company offers a host of life insurance products to the customer with high returns and guaranteed interest payment. Some of the most common plans offered by the company are saving plans, endowment plans, child plans, protection plans and retirement plans. Above this to fulfill the requirements of the customer the company also provides add-on coverages like accidental death benefit rider, accidental total and permanent disability rider and critical illness rider.

Exide Life Insurance Company

Exide Life Insurance Company Limited, is an established and profitable life insurance company, which commenced operations in 2001-02. The Company is head quartered in Bengaluru. It manages assets of INR 18,381 Crores (as on 31 March, 2021). Exide Life Insurance distributes its products through multiple channels viz. Agency, Bancassurance, Corporate Agency & Broking, Direct Channel and Online. The Agency channel comprises of 40,000+ advisors attached to across 200 locations across the country (as on 31 March 2021). The Company offers individual as well as group life insurance solutions.

For more than six decades, Exide Industries has been one of India's most reliable brands, enjoying unrivalled reputation and recall. Constant emphasis on innovation, extensive geographic footprint, strong relationship with marquee clients and steady technology upgradations with global business partners has made Exide Industries, a reliable brand that India trusts. Recognized as the Economic Times Best Brand under the BFSI category in 2020, Exide Life Insurance Company Limited is 100% owned by Exide Industries Limited. One of the pioneers among private life insurers in India, the Company was founded in 2000, and started its operations from 2001.

Funture Generali India Life Insurance Company

Established in year 2007, Future Generali Life Insurance India is a joint venture between Generali Group, Future Group and Industrial Investment Trust Limited. The company has a network of 98 branches over India and since its inception it has sourced over 11 Lakh policies. The company offers one stop solution for all types of financial security to the customer and serves their products on different areas like saving protection, policies and Unit Linked Policies. The policies are offered with a maximum tenure up to 75 years and the eligibility criteria ranges from least 18 years to maximum 56 years.

HDFC Life Insurance Company

HDFC Life Insurance Company India is a joint venture between Housing Development Financial Corporation Ltd. and Standard Life Plus. It was founded in year 2000. The company has currently 27 retail and 8 group products in portfolio. In order to meet the various needs of the customer the company provides an array of individual and group insurance solutions like pension plan, saving and health plan, protection plan, child plan and women plan.

ICICI Prudential Life Insurance Company

ICICI Prudential Life Insurance Company of India is a joint venture between ICICI Bank Ltd.and Prudential Plus. The company began its operation in December 2000 as the first private sector Life insurance in India. For over a decade the company has maintained its top most position amongst the private life insurer in country. To fulfill the different life stage requirements of the customer, ICICI Prudential Life Insurance provides an array of products that enables the buyers to achieve the long term goal. ICICI Prudential life insurance offers products like term plan, ULIP plan, Pension Plan, Child Plan and Investment Plan.

India First Life Insurance Company

The two Indian public sector banks, Bank of Baroda and Andhra Bank went into a joint venture with U.K based investment firm Legal and General and has launched <u>India First Life Insurance</u> Company. Headquartered in Mumbai the company offers investment funds, insurance plans and other policies. The company offers a wide range of plans to cater the need of every individual like saving plans, protection plans, pension plans, term plans and child plans.

Kotak Mahindra Life Insurance Company

Headquartered in Mumbai the J.V between Kotak Mahindra Group and Old Mutual Fund is <u>Kotak Mahindra Life Insurance</u>. Keeping their customers in high priority the company provides a range of term plan, ULIP plan, child plan, saving plan, investment plan, protection plan and retirement plan. The company has much gained name in the market for delivering outstanding value to its customer through customized products and excellent service. The Kotak Mahindra Life Insurance provides plans with a maximum tenure of 30 years and eligibility criteria with minimum 18 years to maximum 65 years.

Life Insurance Corporation (LIC) India Company

Life Insurance Corporation of India knows as LIC of India is one of the most trusted life insurance companies in India. LIC is an Indian state-owned investment corporation and insurance group owned by the Government of India. LIC – The Life insurance corporation of India was established in 1956. More than 250 provident societies and insurance companies were merged to create the state-owned Life

Insurance Corporation of India. On September 1, 1956, the Parliament of India passed the Life Insurance of India Act that nationalized the insurance industry in India.

LIC of India gives you plenty of options when it comes to insurance which help in fulfilling the varied insurance needs of individuals.

The company offers a wide variety of life insurance solutions in India. LIC has various combination of insurance plans such as Money Back Plan, Children Plan, Endowment Plan, Whole Life Plan, Term Plan , Pension Plans, Unit Plans at competitive rates.

Today LIC if India has 25 metro-area service hubs and 54 customer zones located in different cities and towns of India.

LIC functions with 8 zonal offices, 2048 fully computerized branch offices, around 113 divisional offices, 1408 satellite offices, 2,048 branches and the Central Office.

Life Insurance Corporation of India also has a network of 350 Corporate Agents, 1,55,000 individual agents, 120 Brokers, 115 Referral Agents, and 45 Banks for soliciting life insurance business from the public.

Now LIC also has the 1900 branches of Industrial Development Bank of India (IDBI) bank at its disposal. LIC can carry out IDBI's life insurance business through these branches of the bank.

Among the various LIC plans, there are some plans which are the best plan which help in fulfilling the varied insurance needs. Let's first understand the different types of LIC plans:

Take a look at the different types of LIC policy in India by Life Insurance Corporation of India – LIC Of India

Endowment Plan:

The features of endowment plans include the following:

The endowment plans provide guaranteed benefits

If the plan matures, a maturity benefit is paid, a death benefit is paid on death during the policy term

The bonus might be added in the endowment plan

This plan is offered to participate plan

- New Jeevan Anand – (Plan No: 915)
- New Endowment Plan – (Plan No: 914)
- Jeevan Labh – (Plan No: 936)
- Jeevan Lakshya – (Plan No: 933)
- Single-Premium Endowment Plan – (Plan No: 917)
- Aadhaar Stambh – (Plan No: 943)
- New Bima Bachat – (Plan No: 916)
- Aadhaar Shila – (Plan No: 944)

Whole Life Plans

- Bima Shree Policy Document – (Plan No: 948)
- Jeevan Umang – (Plan No: 945)

Money-Back Plans

- New Money Back Plans – 20 YEARS – (Plan No: 920)
- Jeevan Shiromani Policy Document – (Plan No: 947)
- New Children's Money Back Plans – (Plan No: 932)
- New Money Back Plans – 25 YEARS – (Plan No: 921)

- Jeevan Tarun – (Plan No: 934)

Term Assurance Plans

- Term Assurance Plans

- Jeevan Amar – (Plan No: 855)
- Tech Term – (Plan No: 854)
- e-Term Plan

RIDER

- Accidental Death Benefit Rider
- Accident Benefit Rider
- Accidental Death and Disability Benefit Rider
- Critical Illness Benefit Rider
- Premium Waiver Benefit Rider
- Term Assurance Rider

Here you can find business information about Life Insurance Corporation of India such as a business address, products & services, contact Nos., and nature of the business, etc.. At Suger Mint, the company listed in the Investment & Finance Business category.

Life Insurance Corporation of India Registered Office:

Name of Business: Life Insurance Corporation of India – LIC of India

Business Address: Yogakeshema Control Office, Jeevan Bima Marg, Nariman Point

City & Pin Code: Mumbai 400 021

State & Country: Maharastra, India

Toll-free Number & Customer care Number: 18004259876

Business Category: Investment & Finance

Type of Business: Life Insurance Company

Max Life Insurance Company

Max Financial Service Ltd. and Mitsui Sumitomo Insurance Co. Ltd joined hands together and has launched <u>Max Life Insurance</u>. With multi-channel distribution partner and high service providing agencies the company offers the most comprehensive long term protection, saving and retirement schemes. With a strong customer centric approach the company offers one stop solution for all types of insurance and investment needs. Max Life Insurance has a strong track record of 15 years and offers superb investment expertise.

PNB MetLife India Insurance Company

<u>PNB MetLife India Insurance</u> company has over 1,800 corporate clients in India and is spread over 150 different locations in country. The company is well known for its protection and retirement products. Apart from this there are various plans like child plan, saving plan, ULIP plan, Monthly income plan and money back plan that is offered to the customer. PNB MetLife Insurance Company in India came into action in year 2008. For the insurance products offered by the company the eligibility criteria starts from minimum 18 years –maximum 65 years old.

Pramerica Life Insurance Company

Situated in Gurgaon <u>Pramerica Life Insurance</u> company serves with 138 branches and 2586 employees spread across the country. Although despite of being a new company the firm is growing by heaps and bounds and had made a remarkable place in the market. The company offers a variety of plans to the customers within a maximum tenure of 30 years.

Reliance Nippon Life Insurance Company

Reliance Nippon Life Insurance is a part of Reliance capital of the Reliance Group. The company has over 10 million policyholder country wise with a network close to 1,230 branches across the country. Reliance Life Insurance has claim settlement ration of approximately 97.71% and have a record of maximum grievances resolved in 2018-19. The company mainly target products to individuals along with the group sand corporate entities. The company offers range of plans some of the most comprehensive plans like retirement, children, protection, investment and health plan. The maximum tenure of the policies are 35 years and the eligibility criteria to avail the criteria starts from minimum 18 years – maximum 55 years.

Sahara India Life Insurance

Established in 2004, Sahara Life Insurance is India's first wholly owned private life insurance company. With acknowledgeable presence in most part of the country the company serves almost all the sections of the society right from ruler to middle class and urban based. With a customer centric approach the Sahara Life Insurance Provides an extensive range of products like money back plan, unit link plan, term assurance plan, endowment plan and group assurance plan to cater the insurance needs of every individual.

SBI Life Insurance Company

Introduced in year 2001, <u>SBI Life Insurance</u> Company is a Joint venture between State Bank of India and BNP Paribas Cardiff. SBI Life Insurance Company offers an inclusive range of life insurance and pension products at a very economical rate.

Shriram Life Insurance Company

<u>Shriram Life Insurance</u> was established in year 2005, by a joint venture between Shriram Group and Sanlam Group. The company has a network of 630 branches across the different countries in India and caters the diverse needs of the customers from the different cities of the country. The company takes pride for efficient usage of capital and low operation cost. The major key features of the company are that it focuses on ruler market and serve the more economically weaker section of the society. With a variety of plans offered by the company the maximum tenure of the policy ranges up to 25 years and the eligibility criteria ranges from minimum 18 years to maximum 65 years.

Star Union Dai-Ichi Life Insurance Company

The Bank of India, Union Bank of India and life insurance company of Japan Dai-Ichi Life entered into joint venture and has launched <u>Star Union Dai-Ichi Life Insurance</u> Co. Ltd. The company provides a wide range of insurance products to the customers. Star Union Dai-Ichi Life Insurance caters a large number of customers and clients across the country from numerous economic and social background. The company pledges a long term commitment towards their buyers and has earned trust over long years. As a customer centric company, it offers various products like saving plan, wealth plan, protection plan, child plan, pension plan, credit life plan and term plan.

TATA AIA Life Insurance Company

TATA Sons and the AIA Group teamed up to form a joint venture and has launched TATA AIA life Insurance Company. In this venture the majority of stake i.e. 75% is held by TATA Sons and 26 % by AIA Group of company. The company works with a customer centric approach and offers an extensive range of Insurance Product to people, association and corporate insurance buyers. Started working in year 2001 the company provides various plan in multiple segments like group plan, child plan, wealth plan, protection plan, saving plan and micro insurance plan.

Life Insurance Act, 1956:

An Act to provide for the nationalization of life insurance business in India by transferring all such business to a Corporation established for the purpose and to provide for the regulation and control of the business of the Corporation and for matters connected therewith or incidental thereto.

The Life Insurance Act, 1956 was passed by the Parliament on 18th June, 1956, and came into effect from 1st July, 1956.

LIC of India is a Body Corporate having perpetual succession and common seal.

The Life Insurance Corporation having the powers to acquire hold and dispose of property in its own name and can sue and be sued by its own name.

Important Provisions under Life Insurance Corporation Act, 1956 are as follows:

<u>Section 4 of the Life Insurance Act, 1956 deals with the Constitution of the Corporation:</u>

The Corporation shall consist of such number of persons not exceeding sixteen as the Central Government may think fit to appoint thereto and one of them shall be appointed by the Central Government to be the Chairman thereof.

Persons appointing have no such financial interest and other interest.

Section 5 of the Life Insurance Act, 1956 deals with the Capital of the Corporation:

The paid-up equity capital of the Corporation shall be one hundred crore of rupees provided by the Central Government after due appropriation made by Parliament by law for the purpose.

The Corporation may issue and sell bonds and debentures or such other prescribed instruments carrying interest for the purpose of raising its working capital to such amount as may be prescribed.

Section 6 of the Life Insurance Act, 1956 deals with the Functions of the Corporation:

1.Subject to the rules, if any, made by the Central Government in this behalf, it shall be the general duty of the Corporation to carry on life insurance business, whether in or outside India, and the Corporation shall so exercise its powers under this Act as to secure that life insurance business is developed to the best advantage of the community.

2.Without prejudice to the generality of the provisions contained in sub-section (1) but subject to the other provisions contained in this Act, the Corporation shall have power:

a.to carry on capital redemption business, annuity certain business or reinsurance business in so far as such reinsurance business appertains to life insurance business;

b. subject to the rules, if any, made by the Central Government in this behalf, to invest the funds of the Corporation in such manner as the Corporation may think fit and to take all such steps as may be necessary or expedient for the protection or realisation of any investment; including the taking over of and administering any property offered as security for the investment until a suitable opportunity arises for its disposal;

c.to acquire, hold and dispose of any property for the purpose of its business;

d.to transfer the whole or any part of the life insurance business carried on outside India to any other person or persons, if in the interest of the Corporation it is expedient so to do;

e.to advance or lend money upon the security of any movable property or otherwise;

f.to borrow or raise any money in such manner and upon such security as the Corporation may think fit.

g.to carry on either by itself or through any subsidiary any other business in any case where such other business was being carried on by a subsidiary of an insurer whose controlled business has been transferred to and vested in the Corporation under this Act;

h.to carry on any other business which may seen to the Corporation to be capable of being conveniently carried on in connection with its business and calculated directly or indirectly to render profitable the business of the Corporation.

i.to do all such things as may be incidental or conducive to the proper exercise of any of the powers of the Corporation.

3.In the discharge of any of its functions the Corporation shall act so far as may be on business principles.

Section 6A of the Life Insurance Act, 1956 deals with the Power to impose conditions:

1.In entering into any arrangement, under section 6, with any concern, the Corporation may impose such conditions as it may think necessary or expedient for protecting the interest of the Corporation and for securing that the accommodation granted by it is put to the best use by the concern.

2.Where any arrangement entered into by the Corporation under section 6 with any concern provides for the appointment by the Corporation of one or more directors of such concern, such provision and any appointment of directors made in pursuance thereof shall be valid and effective notwithstanding anything to the contrary contained in the Companies Act, 1956 (1 of 1956), or in any other law for the time being in force or in the memorandum, articles of association or any other instrument relating to the concern, and any provision regarding share, qualification, age limit, number of directorships, removal from office of directors and such like conditions contained in any such law or instrument aforesaid, shall not apply to any director appointed by the Corporation in pursuance of the arrangement as aforesaid.

1.Any director appointed as aforesaid shall:

a. hold office during the pleasure of the Corporation and may be removed or substituted by any person by order in writing by the Corporation;

b. not incur any obligation or liability by reason only of his being a director or for anything done or omitted to be done in good faith in the discharge of his duties as a director or anything in relation thereto;

c. not be liable to retirement by rotation and shall not be taken into account for computing the number of directors liable to such retirement.

Section 18 of the Life Insurance Act, 1956 deals with the offices, branches and agencies:

a. Place shall be determined in the official gazette by Central Government.

b. Zonal offices shall establish in Mumbai, Calcutta, Delhi, Kanpur, and Chennai.

c. Territorial limits of each zone may be specified by the Corporation.

Section 19 of the Life Insurance Act, 1956 deals with the Committee of the Corporation:

a. Not more than 5 members execute the committee to exercise all the powers delegated by the Corporation.

b. Investment committee also constitute for advising relating to investment.

c. They may also constitute other committees.

Section 20 to 23 of the Life Insurance Act, 1956 deals with the Authorities under the Act:

Managing Director: The Corporation may appoint one or more persons to be the Managing Director or Directors of the Corporation, and every Managing Director shall be a whole-time officer of the Corporation and shall exercise such powers and perform such duties as may be entrusted or delegated to him by the Executive Committee or the Corporation.

Zonal Managers: The Corporation may entrust the superintendence and direction of the affairs and business of a zonal office to a person whether a member or not, who shall be known as the Zonal Manager and the Zonal Manager shall perform all such functions of the Corporation as may be delegated to him with respect to the area within the jurisdiction of the zonal office.

Corporation may appoint a person as Zonal Manager for the supervision of zonal office.

Zonal Manager also has to perform duties delegated within the jurisdiction of zonal office.

Section 25 to 29 of the Life Insurance Act, 1956 deals with the Finance Accounts and Audit:

As per section 25 of the Act:

1.Auditor Audit the accounts of the Corporation.

2.Auditor appointed by the Corporation with the approval of the Central Government.

3.The Remuneration of the Auditor fixed by the Central Government.

As per section 26 of the Act:

Actuarial Valuation reports to be submit once at least every two years to the Central Government.

As per section 27 of the Act:

Annual report to be prepared at the end of each financial year

As per section 28 of the Act:

If any surplus emerges, ninety per cent or more such surplus, as the Central Government may approve, shall be allocated to or reserved for the life insurance policyholders of the Corporation.

As per section 29 of the Act:

Audit report and report on activities are laid before both the houses of Parliament.

Section 30 of the Life Insurance Corporation Act, 1956 deals with exclusive privilege of carrying on life insurance business:

As per this section Corporation has the Exclusive privilege of carrying on business in India until the certificate of Corporation shall not be cease.

Section 32 of the Life Insurance Corporation Act, 1956 deals with the Power of Corporation to have official seal in certain cases:

The Corporation may have for use in any zonal office, divisional office or in any office outside India an official seal which shall be a facsimile of the common seal of the Corporation, with the addition on its fact of the name of the zonal office, divisional office or other office where it is to be used, and any such official seal may be affixed to any deed or document to which the Corporation is a party.

<u>Section 33 of the Life Insurance Corporation Act, 1956 deals with the requirement of foreign laws to be complied with in certain cases:</u>

Where any property or rights appertaining to the controlled business of an insurer are transferred to and vested in the Corporation under this Act or would be so transferred and vested but for the fact that such transfer and vesting are governed otherwise than by the law of India, the insurer shall comply with such directions as may be given to him by the Corporation for the purpose of securing that the ownership of the property or, as the case may be, that the right is effectively transferred to the Corporation.

<u>Section 37 of the Life Insurance Corporation Act, 1956 deals with the Policies to be guaranteed by Central Government:</u>

The sums assured by all policies issued by the Corporation including any bonuses declared in respect thereof and, subject to the provisions contained in section 14 the amounts assured by all policies issued by any insurer the liabilities under which have vested in the Corporation under this Act, and all bonuses declared in respect thereof, whether before or after the appointed day, shall be guaranteed as to payment in cash by the Central Government.

<u>Section 38 of the Life Insurance Corporation Act, 1956 deals with the Liquidation of Corporation:</u>

The Corporation shall not be placed into liquidation save by order of the Central Government and in such manner the government may direct.

<u>Section 39 of the Life Insurance Corporation Act, 1956 deals with the winding up of certain insurers:</u>

Where any insurer being a company (other than a composite insurer) whose controlled business has been transferred to and vested in the Corporation under this Act has in accordance with the provisions of this Act collected and distributed any moneys paid to him by the Corporation by way of compensation or otherwise and has also complied with any direction given to him by the Corporation for the purpose of securing that the ownership of any property or any right is effectively transferred to the Corporation, the Central Government may on application being made to it in this behalf by such insurer grant a certificate to the insurer that there is no reason for the continued existence of the insurer and where such a certificate has been granted shall cause the certificate to be published in the Official Gazette and upon the publication thereof the insurer shall be dissolved.

<u>Section 40 of the Life Insurance Corporation Act, 1956 deals with the Penalty for Withholding Property:</u>

If any person will fully withholds or fails to deliver to the corporation as required by section 13 be punishable with Imprisonment extended one year or with fine which may extend to one thousand rupees, or with both.

<u>Section 41 of the Life Insurance Corporation Act, 1956 deals with the Tribunal to have exclusive jurisdiction in certain matters:</u>

No Civil Court shall have jurisdiction to entertain or adjudicate upon any matter which the Tribunal is empowered to decide.

CHAPTER FIVE

Life Insurance Act– 1956

An Act to provide for the nationalization of life insurance business in India by transferring all such business to a Corporation established for the purpose and to provide for the regulation and control of the business of the Corporation and for matters connected therewith or incidental thereto.

The Life Insurance Act, 1956 was passed by the Parliament on 18th June, 1956, and came into effect from 1st July, 1956.

LIC of India is a Body Corporate having perpetual succession and common seal.

The Life Insurance Corporation having the powers to acquire hold and dispose of property in its own name and can sue and be sued by its own name.

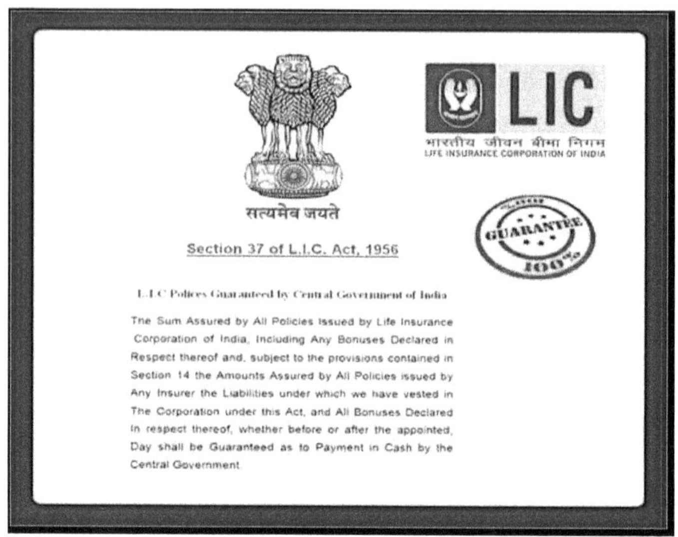

LIC Act 1956

Important Provisions under Life Insurance Corporation Act, 1956 are as follows:

Section 4 of the Life Insurance Act, 1956 deals with the Constitution of the Corporation:

The Corporation shall consist of such number of persons not exceeding sixteen as the Central Government may think fit to appoint thereto and one of them shall be appointed by the Central Government to be the Chairman thereof.

Persons appointing have no such financial interest and other interest.

Section 5 of the Life Insurance Act, 1956 deals with the Capital of the Corporation:

The paid-up equity capital of the Corporation shall be one hundred crore of rupees provided by the Central Government after due appropriation made by Parliament by law for the purpose.

The Corporation may issue and sell bonds and debentures or such other prescribed instruments carrying interest for the purpose of raising its working capital to such amount as may be prescribed.

<u>Section 6 of the Life Insurance Act, 1956 deals with the Functions of the Corporation:</u>

1.Subject to the rules, if any, made by the Central Government in this behalf, it shall be the general duty of the Corporation to carry on life insurance business, whether in or outside India, and the Corporation shall so exercise its powers under this Act as to secure that life insurance business is developed to the best advantage of the community.

2.Without prejudice to the generality of the provisions contained in sub-section (1) but subject to the other provisions contained in this Act, the Corporation shall have power:

a.to carry on capital redemption business, annuity certain business or reinsurance business in so far as such reinsurance business appertains to life insurance business;

b. subject to the rules, if any, made by the Central Government in this behalf, to invest the funds of the Corporation in such manner as the Corporation may think fit and to take all such steps as may be necessary or expedient for the protection or realisation of any investment; including the taking over of and administering any property offered as security for the investment until a suitable opportunity arises for its disposal;

c.to acquire, hold and dispose of any property for the purpose of its business;

d.to transfer the whole or any part of the life insurance business carried on outside India to any other person or persons, if in the interest of the Corporation it is expedient so to do;

e.to advance or lend money upon the security of any movable property or otherwise;

f.to borrow or raise any money in such manner and upon such security as the Corporation may think fit.

g.to carry on either by itself or through any subsidiary any other business in any case where such other business was being carried on by a subsidiary of an insurer whose controlled business has been transferred to and vested in the Corporation under this Act;

h.to carry on any other business which may seen to the Corporation to be capable of being conveniently carried on in connection with its business and calculated directly or indirectly to render profitable the business of the Corporation.

i.to do all such things as may be incidental or conducive to the proper exercise of any of the powers of the Corporation.

3.In the discharge of any of its functions the Corporation shall act so far as may be on business principles.

Section 6A of the Life Insurance Act, 1956 deals with the Power to impose conditions:

1.In entering into any arrangement, under section 6, with any concern, the Corporation may impose such conditions as it may think necessary or expedient for protecting the interest of the Corporation and for securing that the accommodation granted by it is put to the best use by the concern.

2.Where any arrangement entered into by the Corporation under section 6 with any concern provides for the appointment by the Corporation of one or more directors of such concern, such provision and any appointment of directors made in pursuance thereof shall be valid and effective notwithstanding anything to the contrary contained in the Companies Act, 1956 (1 of 1956), or in any other law for the time being in force or in the memorandum, articles of association or any other instrument relating to the concern, and any provision regarding share, qualification, age limit, number of directorships, removal from office of directors and such like conditions contained in any such law or instrument aforesaid, shall not apply to any director appointed by the Corporation in pursuance of the arrangement as aforesaid.

1.Any director appointed as aforesaid shall:

a. hold office during the pleasure of the Corporation and may be removed or substituted by any person by order in writing by the Corporation;

b. not incur any obligation or liability by reason only of his being a director or for anything done or omitted to be done in good faith in the discharge of his duties as a director or anything in relation thereto;

c. not be liable to retirement by rotation and shall not be taken into account for computing the number of directors liable to such retirement.

Section 18 of the Life Insurance Act, 1956 deals with the offices, branches and agencies:

a. Place shall be determined in the official gazette by Central Government.

b. Zonal offices shall establish in Mumbai, Calcutta, Delhi, Kanpur, and Chennai.

c. Territorial limits of each zone may be specified by the Corporation.

Section 19 of the Life Insurance Act, 1956 deals with the Committee of the Corporation:

a. Not more than 5 members execute the committee to exercise all the powers delegated by the Corporation.

b. Investment committee also constitute for advising relating to investment.

c. They may also constitute other committees.

Section 20 to 23 of the Life Insurance Act, 1956 deals with the Authorities under the Act:

Managing Director: The Corporation may appoint one or more persons to be the Managing Director or Directors of the Corporation, and every Managing Director shall be a whole-time officer of the Corporation and shall exercise such powers and perform such duties as may be entrusted or delegated to him by the Executive Committee or the Corporation.

Zonal Managers: The Corporation may entrust the superintendence and direction of the affairs and business of a zonal office to a person whether a member or not, who shall be known as the Zonal Manager and the Zonal Manager shall perform all such functions of the Corporation as may be delegated to him with respect to the area within the jurisdiction of the zonal office.

Corporation may appoint a person as Zonal Manager for the supervision of zonal office.

Zonal Manager also has to perform duties delegated within the jurisdiction of zonal office.

Section 25 to 29 of the Life Insurance Act, 1956 deals with the Finance Accounts and Audit:

As per section 25 of the Act:

1.Auditor Audit the accounts of the Corporation.

2.Auditor appointed by the Corporation with the approval of the Central Government.

3.The Remuneration of the Auditor fixed by the Central Government.

<u>As per section 26 of the Act:</u>

Actuarial Valuation reports to be submit once at least every two years to the Central Government.

<u>As per section 27 of the Act:</u>

Annual report to be prepared at the end of each financial year

<u>As per section 28 of the Act:</u>

If any surplus emerges, ninety per cent or more such surplus, as the Central Government may approve, shall be allocated to or reserved for the life insurance policyholders of the Corporation.

<u>As per section 29 of the Act:</u>

Audit report and report on activities are laid before both the houses of Parliament.

<u>Section 30 of the Life Insurance Corporation Act, 1956 deals with exclusive privilege of carrying on life insurance business:</u>

As per this section Corporation has the Exclusive privilege of carrying on business in India until the certificate of Corporation shall not be cease.

<u>Section 32 of the Life Insurance Corporation Act, 1956 deals with the Power of Corporation to have official seal in certain cases:</u>

The Corporation may have for use in any zonal office, divisional office or in any office outside India an official seal which shall be a facsimile of the common seal of the Corporation, with the addition on its fact of the name of the zonal office, divisional office or other office where it is to be used, and any such official seal may be affixed to any deed or document to which the Corporation is a party.

Section 33 of the Life Insurance Corporation Act, 1956 deals with the requirement of foreign laws to be complied with in certain cases:

Where any property or rights appertaining to the controlled business of an insurer are transferred to and vested in the Corporation under this Act or would be so transferred and vested but for the fact that such transfer and vesting are governed otherwise than by the law of India, the insurer shall comply with such directions as may be given to him by the Corporation for the purpose of securing that the ownership of the property or, as the case may be, that the right is effectively transferred to the Corporation.

Section 37 of the Life Insurance Corporation Act, 1956 deals with the Policies to be guaranteed by Central Government:

The sums assured by all policies issued by the Corporation including any bonuses declared in respect thereof and, subject to the provisions contained in section 14 the amounts assured by all policies issued by any insurer the liabilities under which have vested in the Corporation under this Act, and all bonuses declared in respect thereof, whether before or after the appointed day, shall be guaranteed as to payment in cash by the Central Government.

Section 38 of the Life Insurance Corporation Act, 1956 deals with the Liquidation of Corporation:

The Corporation shall not be placed into liquidation save by order of the Central Government and in such manner the government may direct.

Section 39 of the Life Insurance Corporation Act, 1956 deals with the winding up of certain insurers:

Where any insurer being a company (other than a composite insurer) whose controlled business has been transferred to and vested in the Corporation under this Act has in accordance with the provisions of this Act collected and distributed any moneys paid to him by the Corporation by way of compensation or otherwise and has also complied with any direction given to him by the Corporation for the purpose of securing that the ownership of any property or any right is effectively transferred to the Corporation, the Central Government may on application being made to it in this behalf by such insurer grant a certificate to the insurer that there is no reason for the continued existence of the insurer and where such a certificate has been granted shall cause the certificate to be published in the Official Gazette and upon the publication thereof the insurer shall be dissolved.

<u>Section 40 of the Life Insurance Corporation Act, 1956 deals with the Penalty for Withholding Property:</u>

If any person will fully withholds or fails to deliver to the corporation as required by section 13 be punishable with Imprisonment extended one year or with fine which may extend to one thousand rupees, or with both.

<u>Section 41 of the Life Insurance Corporation Act, 1956 deals with the Tribunal to have exclusive jurisdiction in certain matters:</u>

No Civil Court shall have jurisdiction to entertain or adjudicate upon any matter which the Tribunal is empowered to decide.

CHAPTER SIX

General insurance

Life is full of risks. That's what makes it so interesting and exciting. But some unexpected events can really set you back.

General insurance helps us protect ourselves and the things we value, such as our homes, our cars and our valuables, from the financial impact of risks, big and small – from fire, flood, storm and earthquake, to theft, car accidents, travel mishaps – and even from the costs of legal action against us. And we can choose the types of risks we wish to cover by choosing the right kind of policy with the features we need.

In general, insurance works by spreading the cost of unexpected risks among a large number of people in the same region who share similar risks.

When you take out an insurance policy, you pay a monthly or annual premium. That money joins the premiums of many thousands of other policyholders and goes into a big pool of funds.

With any luck, you will never need to draw on that pool. But if you happen to be one of the unlucky ones affected by an unexpected calamity, perhaps through severe weather or accident, that pool of funds can be used to help you up to the limit you have selected in your policy.

If things go wrong, your insurer may either repair or replace the items that have been lost or damaged, depending on the terms of your policy. You may also have the choice of receiving a cash settlement for the amount of money agreed in your policy.

Q. What is a General Insurance :-

- A policy or agreement between the policyholder and the insurer which is considered only after realization of the premium.
- The premium is paid by the insurer who has a financial interest in the asset covered.
- The insurer will protect the insured from the financial liability in case of loss.

Q. How does the concept of General Insurance work?

Insurance is a concept that applies to a large group of people which may suffer the same risk in the same conditions or region. The money collected as the premium can be called as a pool and when anyone faces a loss, the person is paid from that pool.

Still perplexed at how does a general insurance policy come into play? Consider that your mother suffered a heart attack suddenly and she needs a transplant.

At the same time, your daughter's college fee was due. It definitely is a huge expense to be made at the same time and none can be preferred over the other.

In this time of stress, the family's health insurance policy can save your burden and the fees can be paid from the savings. A General Insurance Policy here works to save your burden for money.

Once we've understood what General Insurance is, let us understand how and when will the policy apply.

Q. A Digit's disclose on how does a loss occur?

The loss may occur due to perils like fire, storm and flood, earthquake, theft, accident, health, travel, and other similar factors.

So now, we know that there exists an asset which is exposed to risk. And in case of the occurrence of losses (subject to the limit of the policy) plays the insurance which pay for the damages.

Q. Why do we need General Insurance?

Imagine you're driving back home in your car and suddenly, a taxi hits you from behind. Your car has a dent and its bumper has come off too. Now you need about Rs. 2000/- for the dent and Rs.7500/- for the bumper to be able to fix it all.

A car insurance policy, in this case, will play well. You can get the amount reimbursed under the insurance policy. Your car is the asset here in which you have a financial interest. But remember, an insurance policy will pay only as per its predefined conditions.

Types of General Insurances in India

Almost everything is insurable. However, General Insurance in India is bifurcated as Fire, Engineering, Marine and Miscellaneous Insurance.

Let us look at them as per the use and general acceptability. Following are the different types of General Insurances in India:

Type of General Insurance

1. **Health Insurance**
2. **Travel Insurance**
3. **Motor Insurance**
4. **Marine Insurance**
5. **Home Insurance**
6. **Commercial Insurance**

Digit Insurance also offers insurance policies for Mobile, Bicycle, Shop Protection, and others.

1. Health Insurance

The Health Insurance cover from Digit offers protection for the medical expenses incurred due to hospitalization caused because of an accident or illnesses.

Although every policy is different, based on who it's being purchased for, it mainly covers:

- Accidental Hospitalization (pre & post)
- Accidental illness and hospitalization
- Daycare procedures
- Psychiatric Support

- Annual Health Checkups
- Daily Hospital Cash

The cover can be extended to cover the following with some predefined conditions:

- Maternity benefit with Infertility benefit
- Critical Illness
- Organ Donation
- AYUSH (Alternate Treatment)

The premium for the health insurance is charged on the basis of:

- Age
- Pre-existing illness
- Lifestyle Habits
- Type of coverage
- Your family health history

2. *Travel Insurance*

Travel Insurance covers your financial liability, if any, when you travel within or beyond the Indian boundaries. The financial liability may arise due to medical or non-medical emergencies.

The duration of the travel for one time can be 180 days at the maximum. The policyholder can take more than one trip in a year. Your Travel Insurance will cover:

- Loss of Baggage
- Loss of Passport

- Hijacking
- Medical Emergencies
- Delayed Flights
- Accidental Deaths
- Adventure Sports

Digit's Travel cover comes with worldwide support and special features like:

- Zero Deductibles.
- Smartphone enabled claim process.
- Customized Travel Plan Cover.
- Missed call claim facilitation.

3. *Motor Insurance*

A Motor Insurance Policy is mandatory to be able to drive legally in India. Broadly there are two types a) Third-Party Liability b) Comprehensive Package Policy.

A Third-Party Policy covers for losses faced in a situation where your vehicle damages any third-party such as a public property, person or third-party vehicle. The same is the minimum requirement to be able to drive legally in India, as stated by the Motor Vehicles Act.

A Comprehensive Package Policy covers both third-party damages and liabilities and damages/losses caused to you and your own vehicle. The losses may arise due to an accident, theft, fire, natural calamities, and others.

Digit Insurance provides some add-ons under its Comprehensive Package Policies for Cars and Bikes that act as additional shields to your vehicle, such as:

- Tyre Protect Cover
- Zero Depreciation Cover
- Return to Invoice
- Engine and Gearbox Protection
- Breakdown Assistance Cover

4. Home Insurance

You build your home with your toil and hard earned money. Everything you buy is a priceless possession for you and hence it needs to be protected.

A Home Insurance Policy protects your valuable and other assets. It is a comprehensive package policy that covers all valuables.

Digit Insurance gives protection for Home against Burglary, Loss/Damage of Jewelry, Fire and Natural Disasters.

5. Commercial Lines

The lines of insurance that affects the business operations in the real terms are categorized under the Commercial Lines of Insurance. Type of the insurance covers that one can buy may include:

- Property Insurance
- Engineering Insurance
- Liability Insurance
- Marine Insurance
- Employees Benefit Insurance
- Business Interruption

Depending on the type of occupation, risk exposure, and the money involved, the insurance could be different for each industry or business.

For example; an insurance that is specific to a cement plant, versus one for an IT company will be different. The premium charged for a cement plant will be higher than a showroom of air conditioner.

Therefore, Insurance is completely based on the level of the risk exposure. A worker in the cement plant is more prone or susceptible to injury than to the one who is working in the showroom.

6. Mobile Insurance

Simple as it reads. A mobile insurance protects the phone from accidental damage. Under the mobile protection cover, Digit Insurance compensates for repair of accidental screen damage to your phone.

The buyers can have mobile insurance for both an old or new phone. Very affordable insurance protection for the most expensive phones you buy.

7. Bicycle Insurance

Not just the cars and two wheelers, people are now passionate for expensive bicycles also. Call it a fashion or change of lifestyle, Bicycle Insurance is another sought product these days. Digit Insurance offers cover against Personal Accident, Theft, Accidental Damage, and Hospital woes.

"Insurance is to manage Cash Flow after a loss occur".

CHAPTER SEVEN

General Insurance Companies

List of General Insurance Companies

Listed below are some of the most prominent general insurance companies catering to the needs of the people from all walks of life:

General Insurance Companies

Aditya Birla General Insurance

Aditya Birla General Insurance provides insurance products along with optimum protection at pocket-friendly rates. It ensures the satisfaction of every individual and the plans are designed in such a way, which fulfils the requirements of the customers. This general insurance company likewise ensures hassle-free and offers smart insurance solutions. Get yourself and your family adequately covered against the uncertainties of life at any point of time.

Bajaj Allianz General Insurance

Bajaj Finserv Limited and Allianz SE joined hands in the year 2001 and formed Bajaj Allianz General Insurance Company. The services offered by the company are IRDA certified and cater to the various insurance needs of the people. This makes it one of the most reliable insurance companies in India. The insurer offers insurance solutions in both life and non-life category. The most famous products include health, travel, motor, home, life insurance etc.

Bharti AXA General Insurance

Bharti AXA General Insurance Company Ltd. is a collaboration of AXA - world pioneer in financial protection and Bharti Enterprise - a leading Indian business group. Established in 2008, the general insurance company is licensed with the Insurance Regulatory and Development Authority of India (IRDA). The insurance provider offers a wide range of general insurance products including health, motor, home, travel, etc.

Cholamandalam MS General Insurance

Cholamandalam MS General Insurance Company Ltd. Is a combined amalgamation between the Murugappa Group and Mitsui Sumitomo. At present, the company has 105 branches across the nation. Besides, the company has a broader product portfolio of motor, accident, travel, rural, and much more accessible for both corporate and individuals.

Digit General Insurance

Digit General Insurance is also known as Go Digit besides is the nation's first digital insurer. The insurer offers a range of non-life insurance products in the category car, two-wheelers, travel, health, home and mobile insurance. The insurer has tie-ups with market leaders such as Policybazaar.com, PayTM, Tanishq, and Cleartrip to ensure a wider audience.

Edelweiss General Insurance

Edelweiss General Insurance assures that that be it you or your family, it will take care of all your insurance needs in terms of the health, the ride or the home where you reside. The USP that makes this a preferred choice amongst the customer is a simplified and quick process of insurance purchase. To enjoy an easy and hassle-free insurance company, Edelweiss Group has surely touched the lives of many. The plans offer caters to the need of all the customers at affordable prices.

Future Generali India General Insurance

Future Generali India is a joint venture between Generali Group and Future Group. The company provides comprehensive insurance solutions through a range of personal, retail, commercial and rural insurance products. Incorporated in 2007, the company was formed with the motive to help its clients to mitigate their financial needs. With more than 15, 00, 00 customers, the insurance provider claims to have settled around 2, 10,000 claims every year. Marking its presence in more than 125 cities in India the various insurance products of the insurer, it offers motor, health, travel, home, PMFBY, lifestyle, commercial, rural etc.

IFFCO Tokio General Insurance

Laid its foundation stone in the year 2000, IFFCO Tokio is collaboration between Tokio Marine, Farmer Fertilizers Co-operative and Nichido Fire Group, a famous fire insurance group in Japan. Since its inception, the insurer has been serving with various non-life insurance products including health, motor, home, travel, SME etc. and is now counted amongst the prominent insurance companies in India.

Kotak Mahindra General Insurance

Kotak Mahindra General Insurance was founded in the year 2015 and a complete subsidiary of Kotak Mahindra Group currently has 13 branches and more across the country. The company ensures customer satisfaction coming from all walks of life and are provided with an array of insurance products such as health, motor, etc. Besides, it also offers different types of third-party liability insurance policy.

Liberty General Insurance

Liberty General Insurance has started its operations in the year 2013. It is a combined agreement between Liberty Mutual Insurance Group, Liberty Industries Limited, and Liberty Citystate Holdings Pte Ltd. The insurer, being one of the competent insurance companies in India strives for providing industrial, commercial and retail insurance solutions. Insurance products like car insurance, two-wheeler insurance, health insurance, and commercial insurance are among the looked for products in the market.

ManipalCigna Health Insurance

ManipalCigna Health Insurance Company Limited (Formerly known as CignaTTK Health Insurance

Company) is a collaboration between Manipal Group, a leader in healthcare delivery and Cigna Corporation, a global health services company. With the motive of spreading wellness and good healthcare, ManipalCigna offers a handful of insurance products ranging from health, travel, personal accident, SME, insurance for employer-employee, and non-employer-employee. The insurer offers quality healthcare and safeguards long term financial goals of its users and hence is one of the leading insurance companies in India.

Max Bupa Health Insurance

Max Bupa Health Insurance Company is a combined venture between Max India Limited and Bupa Finance Plc. based in the UK. In the year 2015, the company has been awarded the prestigious Golden Peacock Award for its flagship product. It has already made a name in the insurance industry with exemplary services and products. With a plethora of choices in the insurance plans, you make a wise choice.

National General Insurance

National Insurance Company started its operations in the year 1906. Headquartered in Kolkata, the insurer offers insurance solutions into various categories including motor, health, home, travel, business etc. Car insurance offered by the insurer is quite famous in the market. It has been rewarded as the Best Auto Insurer in 2017 for car insurance.

Navi General Insurance (formerly known as DHFL General Insurance)

Navi General Insurance (formerly known as DHFL General Insurance) Company offers a diverse product portfolio in regards to travel, motor, health and home insurance. The company essentially focuses upon customers satisfaction and that remains the priority. As per your insurance needs, you can easily tailor the various plans offered by the company and get the maximum coverage.

New India Assurance General Insurance

New India Assurance is a multinational general insurance company of India, which serves in 28 nations and headquartered in Mumbai. The worldwide business of the company is more than Rs. 22,270 Crore. In India, it has 2452 workplaces, including more than 1339 smaller offices. With over 230 products, the insurer believes in providing comprehensive insurance solutions to its customers. The services ranging from insurance in motor, health, travel, rural and marine, the company has been leading the market and remains a preferred choice when it comes to the insurance company in India.

Oriental General Insurance

Headquartered in New Delhi, Oriental General Insurance has been serving this sector since 1947 and has made a mark in the prominent insurance companies in India. With 31 regional offices and more than 1800 operational branches across India, the company offers complete insurance solutions to its customers. Oriental Insurance is not only in India flourishing in India, but also has expanded its services Nepal, Kuwait, and Dubai. Various insurance products offered by the insurer include motor insurance, mediclaim insurance, personal accident insurance, travel insurance, overseas mediclaim insurance, fire insurance, shopkeeper's policy, householder policy etc.

Raheja QBE General Insurance

Raheja QBE is the joint amalgamation of QBE Holdings (AAP) Pty Limited and Prism Cement Limited, India. With the head office in Mumbai, the insurer received its

Certificate of Registration from IRDA in 2008 and is now considered as one of the leading insurance companies in India. Since then, it has been serving the industry with an A+ rating for excellence. The various insurance products offered by the insurer include Health insurance, corporate insurance, health insurance, motor insurance and so on.

Reliance General Insurance

With its 139 branches and more than 28,900 intermediaries all over the country, Reliance General Insurance is one of the renowned names in the list of insurance companies in India. The insurance products offered by the insurer can be categorised into health travel, motor, home marine, etc. The insurer doesn't limit itself to insurance and claims but also encourages the people to follow a healthy standard of living. The company believes in making affordable insurance accessible to all.

Royal Sundaram General Insurance

Royal Sundaram General Insurance, formerly known as Royal Sundaram Alliance Insurance, is the first of its kind to be licensed in October 2000 under IRDA. It holds a rank in the list of foremost insurance companies in India. The insurer was initially a joint venture of Sundaram Finance, a famous non-banking institute and other Indian Shareholders. Ageas Insurance International N.V. acquired 40% of the equity stake and left 10% for Indian Shareholders. The insurer offers a range of insurance products with over 200 employees and 143 branches across the country. The most sought-after products include-car, health home, travel, bike, personal accident, commercial vehicle, business etc.

SBI General Insurance

Founded in the year 2010, SBI General Insurance is a joint venture between two financial giants - State Bank of India (SBI) and Insurance Australia Group (IAG). The insurer offers a range of insurance products in commercial and retail space at affordable premiums and ranks amongst the popular insurance companies in India. The comprehensive range of products includes- health, motor, personal accident, travel, home insurance etc.

Shriram General Insurance

The insurance company is the result of the collaboration between Joint Venture between Shriram Capital Ltd. and Sanlam Limited (South Africa). The insurer started its operations in 2012. The company believes in providing comprehensive insurance solutions through its innovative products in the category car, two-wheelers, travel, home, personal accident, commercial vehicle insurance, business insurance etc

Star Health and Allied Insurance Co Ltd.

Commenced its operations in the year 2006, Star Health and Allied Insurance company have spread its services in health insurance, overseas medical insurance, and personal accident Insurance. The insurer is famous for its service excellence. The insurer offers a wide range of insurance products, whole-heartedly dedicated to health insurance. With a decent claim settlement ratio, it ranks amongst the ideal insurance companies in India.

Tata AIG General Insurance

Headquartered in Mumbai, TATA AIG General Insurance was founded in the year 2001 and is now counted in the foremost insurance companies in India. The company is a result of the collaboration with American International Group and is considered among the sought-after insurance companies. The insurer introduced a range of innovative products to cater to the different needs of its customers. Tata AIG is famous for motor insurance, health insurance, and travel insurance. It also offers insurance to Private Client Group, which includes clients like artists, entrepreneurs and royal families.

United India General Insurance

tarted its operations in the year 1938, United India Insurance Company is one of the finest insurance companies in India. The insurer has its head office in Chennai. Since its inception, the company has emerged leaps and bound to be one of the renowned insurers. Today, it has 18300 workforces spread through 1340 branches across India offering insurance solutions to around 1 Crore policyholders. Ranked amongst the top insurance companies in India, this insurer has a variety of insurance products including motor, health, personal accident, travel, shopkeeper's insurance etc. Among its other product category, there are fire insurance, marine insurance, liability insurance, industrial insurance, credit, micro insurance etc.

Universal Sompo General Insurance

Universal Sompo General Insurance Company Ltd. is a private-public joint venture between three public-sector banks namely, Indian Overseas Bank (IOB), Allahabad Bank, and Karnataka Bank; Dabur India Ltd. - one of the leading FMGC Companies of India, and Sompo Japan Nipponkoa - a private Japanese insurance company based out in Tokyo. Sompo is a Fortune 500 Company that has a capital of 70 Billion Yen. Universal Sompo got 5th position in the list of top 15 for providing general insurance products as per a survey conducted by ICMR-BFM.

CHAPTER EIGHT

Bank Concept

A bank is a financial institution licensed to receive deposits and make loans. Banks may also provide financial services such as wealth management, currency exchange, and safe deposit boxes. There are several different kinds of banks including retail banks, commercial or corporate banks, and investment banks. In most countries, banks are regulated by the national government or central bank.

KEY TAKEAWAYS

- A bank is a financial institution licensed to receive deposits and make loans.
- There are several types of banks including retail, commercial, and investment banks.
- In most countries, banks are regulated by the national government or central bank.

Understanding Banks

Banks are a very important part of the economy because they provide vital services for both consumers and businesses. As financial services providers, they give you a safe place to store your cash. Through a variety of account types such as checking and savings accounts, and certificates of deposit (CDs), you can conduct routine banking transactions like deposits, withdrawals, check writing, and bill payments. You can also save your money and earn interest on your investment. The money stored in most bank accounts is federally insured by the Federal Deposit Insurance Corporation (FDIC), up to a limit of $250,000 for individual depositors and $500,000 for jointly held deposits.1

Banks also provide credit opportunities for people and corporations. The money you deposit at the bank—short-term cash—is used to lend to others for long-term debt such as car loans, credit cards, mortgages, and other debt vehicles. This process helps create liquidity in the market—which creates money and keeps the supply going.

Just like any other business, the goal of a bank is to earn a profit for its owners. For most banks, the owners are their shareholders. Banks do this by charging more interest on the loans and other debt they issue to borrowers than what they pay to people who use their savings vehicles. Using a simple example, a bank that pays 1% interest on savings accounts and charges 6% interest for loans earns a gross profit of 5% for its owners.

Important :- Banks make a profit by charging more interest to borrowers than they pay on savings accounts

Banks range in size based on where they're located and who they serve—from small, community-based institutions to large commercial banks. According to the FDIC there were just over 4,500 FDIC-insured commercial banks in the United States as of 2019.2 This number includes national banks, state-chartered banks, commercial banks, and other financial institutions. While traditional banks offer both a brick-and-mortar location and an online presence, a new trend in online-only banks emerged in the early 2010s. These banks often offer consumers higher interest rates and lower fees. Convenience, interest rates, and fees are some of the factors that help consumers decide their preferred banks.

Special Considerations

U.S. banks came under intense scrutiny after the global financial crisis that occurred in 2007 and 2008. The regulatory environment for banks has since tightened considerably as a result. U.S. banks are regulated at a state or national level. Depending on the structure, they may be regulated at both levels. State banks are regulated by a state's department of banking or department of financial institutions. This agency is generally responsible for regulating issues such as permitted practices, how much interest a bank can charge, and auditing and inspecting banks.

National banks are regulated by the Office of the Comptroller of the Currency (OCC). OCC regulations primarily cover bank capital levels, asset quality, and liquidity. As noted above, banks with FDIC insurance are additionally regulated by the FDIC.

The Dodd-Frank Wall Street Reform and Consumer Protection Act was passed in 2010 with the intention of reducing risks in the U.S. financial system following the financial crisis. Under this act, large banks are assessed on having sufficient capital to continue operating under challenging economic conditions. This annual assessment is referred to as a stress test.3

Types of Banks

- **Retail banks** deal specifically with retail consumers, though some global financial services companies contain both retail and commercial banking divisions. These banks offer services to the general public and are also called personal or general banking institutions. Retail banks provide services such as checking and savings accounts, loan and mortgage services, financing for automobiles, and short-term loans like overdraft protection. Many larger retail banks also offer credit card services to their customers, and may also supply their clients with foreign currency exchange. Larger retail banks also often cater to high-net-worth individuals, giving them specialty services such as private banking and wealth management. Examples of retail banks include TD Bank and Citibank.

- **Commercial or corporate banks** provide specialty services to their business clients from small business owners to large, corporate entities. Along with day-to-day business banking, these banks also provide their clients with other things such as credit services, cash management, commercial real estate services, employer services, and trade finance. JPMorgan Chase and Bank of America are two popular examples of commercial banks, though both have large retail banking divisions as well.

- **Investment banks** focus on providing corporate clients with complex services and financial transactions such as underwriting and assisting with merger and acquisition (M&A) activity. As such, they are known primarily as financial intermediaries in most of these transactions. Clients commonly range from large corporations, other financial institutions, pension funds, governments, and hedge funds. Morgan Stanley and Goldman Sachs are examples of U.S. investment banks.

Unlike the banks listed above, **central banks** are not market-based and don't deal directly with the general public. Instead, they are primarily responsible for currency stability, controlling inflation and monetary policy, and overseeing a country's money supply. They also regulate the capital and **reserve requirements** of member banks. Some of the world's major central banks include the U.S. Federal Reserve Bank, the European Central Bank, the Bank of England, the Bank of Japan, the Swiss National Bank, and the People's Bank of China.

- **PUBLIC SECTOR BANKS**

These banks for more than 75% of the total banking business in the nation. They are called nationalized banks. The government holds the majority stakes at these banks. Post-merger, SBI is the largest public sector banks by volume. It also ranks amongst the top 50 banks in the world.

There are 21 nationalized banks in India, they are:
1. STATE BANK OF INDIA
2. BANK OF INDIA
3. ALLAHABAD BANK
4. BANK OF MAHARASHTRA
5. CANARA BANK
6. INDIAN OVERSEAS BANK
7. IDBI BANK
8. ORIENTAL BANK OF COMMERCE
9. CENTRAL BANK OF INDIA
10. CORPORATION BANK
11. ANDHRA BANK

12. UCO BANK
13. BANK OF BARODA
14. UNION BANK OF INDIA
15. UNITED BANK OF INDIA
16. VIJAYA BANK
17. DENA BANK
18. INDIAN BANK
19. PUNJAB & SIND BANK
20. PUNJAB NATIONAL BANK
21. SYNDICATE BANK

- **PRIVATE SECTOR BANKS**

Private shareholders hold majority stakes in private sector banks. Reserve Bank of India lays down all the rules and regulations. Following are the private sector banks in India:

1. HDFC BANK
2. ICICI BANK
3. AXIS BANK
4. YES BANK
5. INDUSIND BANK
6. KOTAK MAHINDRA BANK
7. DCB BANK
8. BANDHAN BANK
9. IDFC BANK
10. CITY UNION BANK
11. TAMILNAD MERCANTILE BANK
12. NAINITAL BANK
13. CATHOLIC SYRIAN BANK
14. FEDERAL BANK
15. JAMMU AND KASHMIR BANK
16. KARNATAKA BANK

17. DHANALAXMI BANK
18. SOUTH INDIAN BANK
19. LAKSHMI VILAS BANK
20. RBL BANK
21. KARUR VYSYA BANK

- **FOREIGN BANKS**

A bank operating as a private entity in India but headquartered in a Foreign country is a foreign bank. They are governed by both the country they are located in as well the country they have headquarters in. Some of these are:
1. CITI BANK
2. STANDARD CHARTERED BANK
3. HSBC BANK

- **REGIONAL RURAL BANKS**

These banks were established mainly to support the weaker and lesser fortunate section of the society like marginal farmers, laborers, small enterprises etc. they mainly operate at regional levels at different states and may have branches in urban areas as well. Their main features are:
1. Supporting rural and semi-urban region financially
2. Pension distribution and Wage disbursement of MGNREGA workers
3. Added banking facilities like locker, cards-debit, and credit

- **Exchange Banks:**

Exchange banks are mainly deal with international trade. These banks take the responsibility of settlement of foreign exchange and arrange the foreign businesses.

- **SMALL FINANCE BANKS**

These banks cater to a niche segment in the society and help with financial inclusion of sections which are not taken care of by other leading banks. They look after micro industries, unorganized sector, small farmers etc. RBI and FEMA are the governing bodies of these banks.

These are:
1. AU SMALL FINANCE BANK
2. CAPITAL SMALL FINANCE BANK
3. FINCARE SMALL FINANCE BANK
4. EQUITAS SMALL FINANCE BANK
5. ESAF SMALL FINANCE BANK
6. SURYODAY SMALL FINANCE BANK
7. UJJIVAN SMALL FINANCE BANK
8. UTKARSH SMALL FINANCE BANK
9. NORTHEAST SMALL FINANCE BANK
10. JANA SMALL FINANCE BANK

- **PAYMENTS BANK**

This is a new and upcoming model of banking in India. It has been conceptualized and signed-off by RBI with restricted operations. Maximum of Rs. One Lakh is acceptable per customer by these banks. Like other banks, they also offer para-banking services like ATM cards, Debit- Credit cards, net-banking, mobile banking etc

- **Saving Banks:**

Saving banks are those banks which collect and keep the small savings of .the public. They are called thrift promoting institutions. The Saving banks invest the funds in the safest government securities and offer reasonable rate of profit on saving accounts. Students, government employees and household women are usually opening such accounts. A prior notice to bank is necessary for withdrawal of huge amount.

- **Agriculture Banks:**

The bank is responsible for the development of agriculture sector of the country. Agriculture banks are set tip to provide financial assistance to the agriculturists and agro-based industries.

- **Industrial Banks:**

The Industrial banks provide medium and long-term credit to the industries. The growth of industries depends on these banks.

- **Export-Import Banks:**

The bank which is related to export and import finance of the country is called export import bank.

- **School Banks:**

This type of bank offers special financial feature for the schools. This bank also gives loans to the administration.

- **Central Bank:**

Central Bank is the bank of banks. Every civilized country now has its own central bank. The primary function of the central bank is to regulate the flow of money and credit in order to promote efficiency, stability and growth in the country.

Bank vs. Credit Union

Credit unions vary in size from small, community-based entities to larger ones with thousands of branches across the country. Just like banks, credit unions provide routine financial services for their clients who are generally called members. These services include deposit, withdrawal, and basic credit services.

But there are some inherent differences between the two. While a bank is a profit-driven entity, a credit union is a nonprofit organization traditionally run by volunteers. Created, owned, and operated by participants, they are generally tax-exempt. Members purchase shares in the coop, and that money is pooled together to provide a credit union's credit services. Because they are smaller entities, they tend to provide a limited range of services compared to banks. They also have fewer locations and automated teller machines (ATMs).

Types of Bank Accounts

The common types of bank accounts include:

1. Savings account

A savings account is a bank account that a customer can deposit money in that they do not need right away, but that is available for withdrawal whenever needed. The bank loans out the money to borrowers and charges interest on the amount of credit disbursed.

2. Checking account

A checking account allows customers to access their deposited funds with ease, and they can use it to make their financial transactions such as paying bills. A customer can access the funds by writing a check, using a debit card to withdraw money or make payments, or by setting up automatic transfers to another account.

3. Certificate of deposit

A certificate of deposit is a bank account that holds a fixed amount of money for a defined period of time such as six months, one year, two years, etc. It pays a fixed interest rate on the amount held.

Principles of Banking

1. Liquidity:

Liquidity is an important principle of bank lending. Bank lend for short periods only because they lend public money which can be withdrawn at any time by depositors. They, therefore, advance loans on the security of such assets which are easily marketable and convertible into cash at a short notice.

A bank chooses such securities in its investment portfolio which possess sufficient liquidity. It is essential because if the bank needs cash to meet the urgent requirements of its customers, it should be in a position to sell some of the securities at a very short notice without disturbing their market prices much. There are certain securities such as central, state and local government bonds which are easily saleable without affecting their market prices.

The shares and debentures of large industrial concerns also fall in this category. But the shares and debentures of ordinary firms are not easily marketable without bringing down their market prices. So the banks should make investments in government securities and shares and debentures of reputed industrial houses.

2. Safety:

The safety of funds lent is another principle of lending. Safety means that the borrower should be able to repay the loan and interest in time at regular intervals without default. The repayment of the loan depends upon the nature of security, the character of the borrower, his capacity to repay and his financial standing.

Like other investments, bank investments involve risk. But the degree of risk varies with the type of security. Securities of the central government are safer than those of the state governments and local bodies. And the securities of state government and local bodies are safer than those of the industrial concerns. This is because the resources of the central government are much higher than the state and local governments and of the latter higher than the industrial concerns.

In fact, the share and debentures of industrial concerns are tied to their earnings which may fluctuate with the business activity in the country. The bank should also take into consideration the debt repaying ability of the governments while investing in their securities. Political stability and peace and security are the prerequisites for this.

It is very safe to invest in the securities of a government having large tax revenue and high borrowing capacity. The same is the case with the securities of a rich municipality or local body and state government of a prosperous region. So in making investments the bank should choose securities, shares and debentures of such governments, local bodies and industrial concerns which satisfy the principle of safety.

Thus from the bank's viewpoint, the nature of security is the most important consideration while giving a loan. Even then, it has to take into consideration the creditworthiness of the borrower which is governed by his character, capacity to repay, and his financial standing. Above all, the safety of bank funds depends upon the technical feasibility and economic viability of the project for which the loan is advanced

3. Diversity:

In choosing its investment portfolio, a commercial bank should follow the principle of diversity. It should not invest its surplus funds in a particular type of security but in different types of securities. It should choose the shares and debentures of different types of industries situated in different regions of the country. The same principle should be followed in the case of state governments and local bodies. Diversification aims at minimising risk of the investment portfolio of a bank.

The principle of diversity also applies to the advancing of loans to varied types of firms, industries, businesses and trades. A bank should follow the maxim: "Do not keep all eggs in one basket." It should spread it risks by giving loans to various trades and industries in different parts of the country.

4. Stability:

Another important principle of a bank's investment policy should be to invest in those stocks and securities which possess a high degree of stability in their prices. The bank cannot afford any loss on the value of its securities. It should, therefore, invest it funds in the shares of reputed companies where the possibility of decline in their prices is remote.

Government bonds and debentures of companies carry fixed rates of interest. Their value changes with changes in the market rate of interest. But the bank is forced to liquidate a portion of them to meet its requirements of cash in cash of financial crisis. Otherwise, they run to their full term of 10 years or more and changes in the market rate of interest do not affect them much. Thus bank investments in debentures and bonds are more stable than in the shares of companies.

5. Profitability:

This is the cardinal principle for making investment by a bank. It must earn sufficient profits. It should, therefore, invest in such securities which was sure a fair and stable return on the funds invested. The earning capacity of securities and shares depends upon the interest rate and the dividend rate and the tax benefits they carry. It is largely the government securities of the centre, state and local bodies that largely carry the exemption of their interest from taxes. The bank should invest more in such securities rather than in the shares of new companies which also carry tax exemption. This is because shares of new companies are not safe investments

Commercial Bank principles

1. Principle of Liquidity

The principle of liquidity is very important for the commercial bank. Liquidity refers to the ability of an asset to convert into cash without loss within a short time.

Paying the deposited money on demand of customers is called liquidity in the sense of banking.

2. Principle of Solvency

Solvency means financial capability or sufficiency in the capital. To stay in these competitive market commercial banks must have sufficient capital. If the funds are not sufficient the bank cannot run his business.

The main source of funds of the commercial bank is the deposited money by the depositors through the different types of accounts.

Depositors keep cash in the bank, especially for safety. So commercial banks must ensure the safety of deposited funds.

3. Principle of Profitability

The main objective of the commercial bank is to earn a profit.

For earning profit commercial bank have to invest by providing short-term loans, before providing loan commercial banks have to compensate a certain amount of money as liquidity.

4. Principle of Loan and Investment

The main source of profit of bank is granting loans to any individual or organization. Investment is a profitable and sound source of income. Commercial banks invest in the business and investment sectors.

5. Principle of Savings

Commercial banks collect funds by creating savings facilities. Commercial banks try to collect savings from society surplus.

The commercial bank invests these savings to generate profit. So, more savings, more investment, and more profit.

6. Principle of Services

The commercial bank ensures the best services to their customers. The success of a bank depends on the services provided by the bank. The customer chooses those banks that provide improved services.

7. Principle of Secrecy

Customers want to keep secrets about their valuable assets and money.

So banks must have to keep secrets about their customer's accounts. If a commercial bank does not maintain secrecy the customer will be dissatisfied.

8. Principle of Efficiency

The commercial bank should operate their business efficiently. So that they can succeed at the objective.

In this competitive market, there is no alternative way without efficiency in management. So commercial bank must train their employees to increase the efficiency in management.

9. Principle of Location

Commercial banks must have to locate their branches in the commercial area where many customers are available. The location must be safe for the customers and an easy communication system must exist.

Other principles;

- **The principle of goodwill.**
- **The principle of the economy.**
- **The principle of technology.**
- **The principle of publicity.**

Objectives of Bank

A bank is a financial institution. It is one kind of financial institution which deals with money and other monetary instruments and conducts business. Bank receives deposits from one group of people and lends it to other groups of people. By this process, the bank earns a profit. Profit is the main objective of a bank. But a bank is different from other financial institution. So, its objectives are also different in some factors. Here we discussed some objectives of bank,

Marketing profit

Marketing profit is the main task of all banks except the central bank. Bask creates profit from money transaction. Bank takes more interest from debtor than give interest to depositors. The difference between these two makes a profit for Bank.

Issuing Notes

The Central bank has the sole power to issue the note. Other banks make the availability of note in the market. No other Bank can issue note.

Controlling of money market

The most fundamental duty of central bank is to control the money market. For this, it has to take help from other commercial banks. To control money market central bank and other bank have to work jointly.

Creating utility of currency

To make utility currency commercial banks always work actively. Several kinds of monetary instruments are used by banks to create utility and speed up the flow of the economy.

Rendering service

Commercial banks render service to people by various activities. By serving people banks earn the profit and increase goodwill.

Taking deposits and giving loan

Deposit is the lifeblood of a bank and the lending is the life-supporting main function of the bank. So the bank is established to take a deposit from one group of people and lend it to another group.

Economic development

Bank and the economic development are inter-related to each other. Basically, bank increase the credit creation, infrastructural development, internal trade financing, remittance etc., those are the indicator of the economic development.

Dealing in foreign exchange

Bank deals with the foreign exchange as the authorized dealer. They purchase and sell foreign currencies to the intending sellers and the buyers at the market rates.

Development of standard at living

Bank helps people to make their life easy, flexible, and standard. It gives standard salary to its employees. Bank gives loan to many types of commercial sectors for the development.

The bank has the principle and the ancillary functions that create the significant role of the bank. Above discussed points must be followed by the bank to sustain and to create goodwill in the market so sophistically comparing to the core competitors

Important Functions of Bank

There are two types of functions of banks:

- **Primary functions** – being primary are also called banking functions.
- **Secondary Functions**

Both the types of functions of bank are explained below in detail:

Primary Functions of Bank

All banks have to perform two major primary functions namely:

1. Accepting of deposits
2. Granting of loans and advances

1. **Accepting of Deposits** A very basic yet important function of all the commercial banks is mobilising public funds, providing safe custody of savings and interest on the savings to depositors. Bank accepts

different types of deposits from the public such as:

2. **Saving Deposits**: encourages saving habits among the public. It is suitable for salary and wage earners. The rate of interest is low. There is no restriction on the number and amount of withdrawals. The account for saving deposits can be opened in a single name or in joint names. The depositors just need to maintain minimum balance which varies across different banks. Also, Bank provides ATM cum debit card, cheque book, and Internet banking facility. Candidates can know about the Types of Cheques at the linked page.

3. **Fixed Deposits**: Also known as Term Deposits. Money is deposited for a fixed tenure. No withdrawal money during this period allowed. In case depositors withdraw before maturity, banks levy a penalty for premature withdrawal. As a lump-sum amount is paid at one time for a specific period, the rate of interest is high but varies with the period of deposit.

4. **Current Deposits**: They are opened by businessmen. The account holders get an overdraft facility on this account. These deposits act as a short term loan to meet urgent needs. Bank charges a high-interest rate along with the charges for overdraft facility in order to maintain a reserve for unknown demands for the overdraft.

5. **Recurring Deposits**: A certain sum of money is deposited in the bank at a regular interval. Money can be withdrawn only after the expiry of a certain period. A higher rate of interest is paid on recurring deposits as it provides a benefit of compounded rate of interest and enables depositors to collect a big sum of money. This type of account is operated by salaried persons and petty traders.

2. **Granting of Loans & Advances** The deposits accepted from the public are utilised by the banks to advance loans to the businesses and individuals to meet their uncertainties. Bank charges a higher rate of interest on loans and advances than what it pays on deposits. The difference between the lending interest rate and interest rate for deposits is bank profit.

Bank offers the following types of Loans and Advances:

1. **Bank Overdraft**: This facility is for current account holders. It allows holders to withdraw money anytime more than available in bank balance but up to the provided limit. An overdraft facility is granted against collateral security. The interest for overdraft is paid only on the borrowed amount for the period for which the loan is taken.

2. **Cash Credits**: a short term loan facility up to a specific limit fixed in advance. Banks allow the customer to take a loan against a mortgage of certain property (tangible assets and / guarantees). Cash credit is given to any type of account holders and also to those who do not have an account with a bank. Interest is charged on the amount withdrawn in excess of the limit. Through cash credit, a larger amount of loan is sanctioned than that of overdraft for a longer period.

3. **Loans**: Banks lend money to the customer for short term or medium periods of say 1 to 5 years against tangible assets. Nowadays, banks do lend money for the long term. The borrower repays the money either in a lump-sum amount or in the form of instalments spread over a pre-decided time period. Bank charges interest on the

actual amount of loan sanctioned, whether withdrawn or not. The interest rate is lower than overdrafts and cash credits facilities.

4. **Discounting the Bill of Exchange**: It is a type of short term loan, where the seller discounts the bill from the bank for some fees. The bank advances money by discounting or purchasing the bills of exchange. It pays the bill amount to the drawer(seller) on behalf of the drawee (buyer) by deducting usual discount charges. On maturity, the bank presents the bill to the drawee or acceptor to collect the bill amount.

Secondary Functions of Bank

Like Primary Functions of Bank, the secondary functions are also classified into two parts:

1. Agency functions
2. Utility Functions

1. **Agency Functions of Bank** Banks are the agents for their customers, hence it has to perform various agency functions as mentioned below:

Transfer of Funds: Transfering of funds from one branch/place to another.

Periodic Collections: Collecting dividend, salary, pension, and similar periodic collections on the clients' behalf.

Periodic Payments: Making periodic payments of rents, electricity bills, etc on behalf of the client.

Collection of Cheques: Like collecting money from the bills of exchanges, the bank collects the money of the cheques through the clearing section of its customers.

Portfolio Management: Banks manage the portfolio of their clients. It undertakes the activity to purchase and sell the shares and debentures of the clients and debits or credits the account.

Other Agency Functions: Under this bank act as a representative of its clients for other institutions. It acts as an executor, trustee, administrators, advisers, etc. of the client.

Utility Functions of Bank:-

- Issuing letters of credit, traveller's cheque, etc.
- Undertaking safe custody of valuables, important documents, and securities by providing safe deposit vaults or lockers.
- Providing customers with facilities of foreign exchange dealings
- Underwriting of shares and debentures
- Dealing in foreign exchanges
- Social Welfare programmes
- Project reports
- Standing guarantee on behalf of its customers, etc.

CHAPTER NINE

Concept of Bank Management

There are many definitions of bank management. In general, bank management refers to the process of managing the Bank's statutory activity. Bank management is characterized by the specific object of management - financial relations connected with banking activities and other relations, also connected with implementation of management functions in banking.

The main objective of bank management is to build organic and optimal system of interaction between the elements of banking mechanism with a view to profit.

Successful optimization of the "profitability-risk" ratio in a bank lending operations is largely determined by the use of effective methods of bank management. Ability to take reasonable risk is one of the elements of entrepreneurship culture in general and banking culture in particular.

Reliability of the bank management is determined by the following characteristics:

i. management expertise in strategic analysis, planning, policy development and management functions;

v. quality of planning;

v. risk management (credit, interest rate and currency risks);

v. liquidity management;

v. management of human resources;

v. creation of control systems: audit and internal audit , monitoring of profitability and risks liquidity;

v. unified information technology system: integrated automation of workflow, accounting, current analysis and control, strategic planning.

All the above conditions show themselves during implementation of bank management and its components.

OR

Banks create funds through collecting surplus savings as deposits or the capital of shareholders or taking loans from other sources, including the central bank. To collect these funds, a bank has to bear some collection_cost and other related costs. After deducting the cost of funds and other administrative expenses, a bank has to profit by collecting funds and investing the same to become an efficient and successful bank.

For building a professional management brigade, a bank needs to select an appropriate organizational structure to do its activities. The process of bank management is described below as a circle. But the management process starts from planning, followed by organization, coordination, motivation, and control. Ideal management can be ensured by the proper coordination of all these elements.

According to Peter F. Drucker, "The manager has the task of creating a true whole that is larger than the sum of us parts, a productive entity that turns out more than the sum of the resources pul into it."

Importance of Bank Management – Rationale of Increasing Importance of Bank Management

Bank's management procedure is more challenging as the regulatory system always is there to control the bank management.

1. Changing Regulation of Banks.
2. Increasing Competition due to Changing Technological Development.
3. Changing International Relationship.

1. Changing Regulation of Banks

At the end of the 3rd decade of the 20th century, thousands of banks worldwide failed due to the economic recession called Great Depression.

Due to the bank failure, millions of depositors suffered from a great problem, as they didn't get back their deposited money. To protect the interest of depositors, the deposit insurance scheme was made mandatory for banks.

And from this time, the regulation for banks began to multiply from various angles.

Previously, receiving a registration certificate or certificate of commencement of business and submitting the financial statements were considered sufficient for the controlling agencies of banks.

Some of the techniques followed by the bank regulatory authorities to control the activities of commercial banks are;

- Direction for the right price of bank services.
- Introduction of deposit insurance.
- Direction for adequate liquidity.

- Direction for capital adequacy.
- Direction for approval and non-approval of bank loan operation.
- Recruitment of directors and direction regarding recruitment and directing their duties and responsibilities.
- Loan supervision, review, and examination.
- Direction for adequacy reserve etc.
- Day by day, bank management becomes more challenging by introducing rules and regulations by bank regulatory authorities.

2. Increasing Competition due to Changing Technological Development

The number of served clients and quality dimensions of services is the basis of competition. The bank, which provides better service with high quality, is capable of being successful in competition.

Two banks jointly create new services that provide the customers with a sustainable competitive advantage.

Why the new benefit or service that the bank offer is unique and different from that of the other organizations requires the commercial banks to participate in the multidimensional competitive environment.

The bank, which can attract more clients, can create clients repeatedly. This technological environment absorbed more investment and new training.

So, the bank's management creates a new strategy of banking services adjusted in the competitive banking business.

3. Changing International Relationship

In the international banking business, the bank faces an extensive amount of legislation in the event of a new problem. International relations, global or bilateral, create more competition in the banking business.

Other factors, such as international trade and commerce, laws of found transfer, changes in social and cultural factors, establish a new operational management system that challenges the banking business.

In this era of modern science, a solution of competitive environment and development of international relations among banks, the bank's management follows a strategy to merge banks in the international banking business.

All these factors stated make bank management more complex and challenging.

Other Importance

v.   It involves the regulation of service fees and charges

v.   It manages approval and disapproval of bank loan operations

v.   It manages bank reserve

v.   It supervises the recruitment of directors

v.   It controls the issuance of deposits

v.   It identifies a suitable location for bank operations

v.   It ensures capital adequacy

Elements in bank management are;

1.   Planning
2.   Objectives
3.   Policies
4.   Rules
5.   Strategy
6.   Communication
7.   Organizing
8.   Coordinating

9. Motivating
10. Controlling
11. Reports
12. Audit
13. Examination

1. Planning

The bank management process starts with planning. Planning is the activity through which a business firm charts its future course of action. In bank management, planning gives answers to the questions related to a bank as a whole or a particular branch, or a particular work division. These questions can be like

v. What role to be performed by a bank, branch, or work division?
v. How does a work division contribute to the activities of other work divisions?
v. What type of activities is the bank engaged in?
v. Is the bank providing any exceptional services?

The second step of planning is to set long-term and short-term goals. One point must be remembered here we are not talking about the separate long-term and short-term planning. Rather a plan with the combination and coordination of body long term and short term goals is considered here.

The long-term goals of banks identify some overall topics, which are achievable in the future. For example

v. What will be the optimum scope and size of the bank in some future period of time?

v. What type of efforts would be taken to develop new market segments?

v. What type of loan assets will comprise the future loan portfolio of banks?

v. What will be the size of a specific work division in the future?

Short-term goals of planning describe the targets achievable shortly elaborately. A budget is attached to this part of the planning.

Some techniques and tools are helpful for planning. Management by objective (MBO) is one of those. MBO can not help planning automatically. But in the hand of an efficient bank manager, it acts as a strong and unique tool.

Planning is the activity through which a business firm charts its future course of action. The result of planning is to develop a strategy for utilizing the resources of a business within its projected environment to attain its overall objectives.

Many banks realize the importance of this function and have planning departments staffed with technical personnel. Others do it intermittently.

1. Objectives

Objectives are goals, and it is toward these results that all activities are directed. Objectives may change over time, but once formulated, they are looked upon as firm and binding contracts. Bank objectives are usually stated in short, concise terms and limited to ten to twelve items. A few items from a list of one bank s objectives follow:

1. Our business is selling financial services in Oregon and in selected regional, national, and international markets. We will extend our business into areas that provide sound expansion opportunities meeting predetermined profit criteria.
2. We will strive for stability in earning growth, acquiring high-quality investments, and pursuing sound and innovative tactics '. Through strategic planning and strong management, we will aggressively expand income sources while remaining in control of costs.
3. Our primary marketing objective is to increase our market share through superior service and appropriate products consistent with corporate strategic plans.
4. Management will provide continuity of policies and directions. Changes will be implemented quickly and in a manner that considers both individual and corporate needs.
5. Our objective is to promote people within the organization. However, expansion into new fields and the need for specialized talent may require hiring people from other sources.
6. We are sensitive to social and economic concerns and recognize our responsibilities as corporate citizens. We support and participate in activities to improve social and economic conditions.

2. Policies

After the setting of objectives, the establishment of bank policies naturally follows. Policies are general statements of understandings that are designed to stimulate thinking and action in decision making. An example of a bank policy might involve pricing. Policies assist those people who are concerned with planning.

It is difficult to conceive of the preparation of a budget without the knowledge of the overall policies. Policies also serve as an overall guide or boundaries within which the officers and committees of a bank can operate.

If a set of circumstances arises, the bank has a policy or a determined course of action upon which it can rely for guidance. The policy acts as a coordinating force to call forth group effort Policies may appear in the minutes of the board of directors or standing committees or die manual of organization.

3. Rules

Rules should not be confused with policies. A rule requires that specific and definitive actions be taken or not taken for a given situation. A bank may require that a corporation opening an account provide the bank with a resolution prepared by die firm's board of directors authorizing certain individuals to sign checks and borrow funds. This would be a rule.

4. Strategy

Once a bank's objectives and policies are formulated, the next step is to arrive at a strategy to accomplish these goals and objectives. While objectives represent a subjective choice as to the quality, direction, and pace of the enterprise, strategy is the plan by which a bank can best realize the established objectives

5. Communication

One of the problems in any business firm is communicating the established objectives, policies, and rules of operation to all who need them, and banking is no exception.

Rules of operation are essential to banking because of bank regulatory authorities' many rules and regulations.

Banks' senior officers are usually in close daily contact, and the knowledge of various developments does not present a major problem. The same is true of lending officers who work closely together and are concerned with specific types of lending, such as commercial and consumer loans.

Communication channels must dept open in branch and group banking organizations and among the numerous clerks, tellers, bookkeepers, computer operators, and others widely dispersed throughout the organization.

6. Organizing

Organizational structure is the extra strength of hank management under the umbrella of planning. After setting the objectives and rules, necessary components are organized to achieve the goal.

Louis A Allen says. "The process of identifying and grouping the work to be performed, defining and delegating responsibility and authority, and establishing relationship to enable people to work most efficiently together in accomplishing the objectives."

Earnest Dale says, "Organization is the structural process in which individuals interact for achieving the stated objectives." ,

The main objective of organizational activities is to earn expected profit. Other factors of production can be integrated effectively and efficiently by organizations to achieve the expected goal.

If every person of an organization docs their own duties according to the established plan, their combined activities make a bank achieve its goals. If the duty of every person is not defined properly, the organizational activities become slow, confusing, and ineffective.

If what is to be done is not clear, it becomes almost impossible to achieve the targeted goals. Again without well-defined goals, organizational activities are impossible. We can organize the activities of banks according to types, divisions, geographical areas, floors, etc

Organizational activities can be defined by the scale of work description and work completion. A manager does all the duties to achieve the goal. But they will be accountable for their work areas. The organizational concept depends on the concept of labor segmentation.

A person should be given proper authority within their accountable work-areas. This is called delegation of authority. Assigned work makes new responsibility to be accountable for the work. Authority docs do not increase or decrease the responsibility which was assigned before. So authority can be delegated, but responsibility and accountability can never be delegated.

By delegating authority, administrative decentralization is made. This decentralization works more when a manager limits the delegated authority by law, rules, moral responsibility, and budget.

The summary is organization is related to a human being. It is created through interpersonal relationships. The nature of human beings influences the organization. So. all the tools and rules for developing human capital in a bank help a manager develop an organizational system.

7. Coordinating

Coordination means working together. Because group skill is the maximum considerable issue in coordination, but we should also keep in mind that some freedom is essential for creativity.

So the right decision should be taken at in right time through proper coordination. Coordination was due importance in bank management for a long time. Different types of business activities, departments, divisions, and personalities of the organization, if not methodically coordinated, will result in low performance and confusion in implementing planned activities.

When the authority is delivered after an organization is divided into different managerial units, each unit starts to work as an autonomous organization. According to effective planning, a predefined general goal helps organize the activities of different groups of an organization only when properly coordinated.

But if the organizational structure becomes complex, it will be challenging to organize different groups based on general goals.

Every department enjoys some autonomous power and facilities according to the norms of the management process. As every department is a part of the bank, relationship building among the departments is essential for undertaking the right approach in realizing the bank's goals in general and the unit in particular.

Every bank manager is basically a coordinator. They play an important role by directing and helping the personnel working under his management area. As a coordinator, they coordinate the work of their subordinates in the group with other groups of the bank or other groups outside the bank.

When a bank manager is assigned with mid-level or lower-level management, he may find it difficult to make a relationship between an unrelated work with their department's goals. But a manager should motivate his people to coordinate with that work. For ease of coordination, different types of tools are used. Communication is one of them.

In the case of communication, honesty is necessary. The flow of information will be effective if a manager is honest in providing training to their subordinates. Employee and work-schedule coordination ability is the pre-requisite of a successful manager. A successful manager adjusts with the personal goal of the employees and the organizational goals through guidance, counseling, and direction.

8. Motivating

Motivation is the most discussed issue of the bank officials and bank management process. It is the key to employees' work performance with the required efficiency. Group activities at)d satisfaction depend on it. Basically, the human being is the source of their own motivation. A bank manager helps to create some stimuli among the employees to be self-motivated.

A bank manager should be concerned about the high ambition of human beings. Work satisfaction is the prerequisite of success. On the other hand, work success influences work satisfaction. Every efficient manager has to find out some ways so that employees can assess their success. There are different ways of self-assessment: for example –

• Evaluation

- Appraisal
- Performance review
- Merit rating

Each of these has two basic procedures:

1. Evaluation for quality improvement
2. Evaluation to remove weaknesses

In every organization, such systems should be established, which will help die employees to judge themselves logically. A manager has to use the assessment tools properly. Besides determining the evaluation criteria, banks should ensure a positive & neutral evaluation system to establish efficient management. If the assessment is unbiased and friendly to overcome the weak side of the employees, they will be motivated to work properly.

The prize, honorarium & remuneration, medals, promotion, transfer to preferred place, training, travel and lours, etc., are some tools popularly used to raise motivation. A good reward system is necessary to encourage and acknowledge the contribution of self-motivated managers.

Most people want success in their professional life. So an efficient manager gives freedom to subordinates to reach a better position. Because they know that the highly skilled employees may change die job to achieve more professional development and reach a better position.

In this way, managers try to improve the work efficiency of die employees by giving freedom to reach better professional position. Effective motivation not only raises productivity but also reduces employee turnover to a great extent.

9. Controlling

Of all the functions of management in banking, probably the most thoroughly executed is controlling. The reason stems from the role that commercial banks play in our society.

Banks, more than any other industry, rely on public confidence. Banks hold die bulk of the cash balances of the nation and are closely regulated by bank regulatory agencies that have spawned a multitude of rules and regulations. High standards and accuracy are expected of them.

10. Reports

There are many avenues for control in commercial banks. Banks are noted for the multitude of information systems made possible by the computer age and the consumption of tons of paper. There seem to report available on every function.

11. Audit

Many banks have an audit department, and that does not normally employ an outside accounting Finn to perform a periodic audit of the bank. Auditing is concerned with reviewing transactions for accuracy and determining whether such transactions have been recorded in conformity with accepted accounting principles and banking regulations.

12. Examination

Excellent external control is the bank examination. Federal and or state regulatory authorities usually examine a bank once a year and those in financial difficulties more often.

The objective of bank management:

The main objective of bank management is to maximize the profit of the bank maintaining proper management of liquidity, asset, liability and capital adequacy. For achieving this, banks must strictly follow some standards and organized system.

Other objectives of bank management include

- To meet the challenges of the changing environment
- To improve customer service
- To introduce a new scheme
- To improve housekeeping
- To cope up with new technology for bank
- To modernize office equipment
- To train employees on a regular basis
- To improve work ethics
- To improve the overall health of the bank
- To improve organizational culture and value system
- To improve corporate social responsibility.
- To improve productivity through participative management
- To improve inspection and special audit
- To follow the instructions and stick to rules and guidelines
- To improve the human resources of the bank

Functions of bank management:

Following are the major functions of bank management

v.   Deposit mobilization
v.   Financial management
v.   Project evaluation
v.   Credit management
v.   Credit planning
v.   Liquidity management
v.   Investment management
v.   Organizational management
v.   Marketing management
v.   Office management
v.   Maintainance management
v.   Information management
v.   Legal management
v.   Portfolio management
v.   Assets management

CHAPTER TEN

Legal Framework of regulation of bank

Legal Framework

The Indian banking system is primarily governed by Banking Regulation Act, 1949. The Reserve Bank of India Act, 1934 empowers the RBI (Reserve Bank of India) to act on a wide range of issues including rules, regulations, directions and guidelines with respect to banking and financial services. The RBI is the central bank of India.

Besides the above, the FEMA (Foreign Exchange Management Act, 1999) regulates with respect to cross-border transactions.

Reserve Bank of India (RBI)

The primary regulator for banks in India is RBI. The functions of RBI include:

- Making norms for opening up and licensing banks (including foreign bank branches in India)
- Corporate governance and organization
- Norms for various products and services
- Finalizing monetary policy

- Regulation of foreign exchange, government securities markets and financial derivatives
- Government debt and cash management
- Overseeing payment and settlement systems
- Currency Management
- To liaise with other financial sector regulators like SEBI, IRDAI etc. RBI needs to regulate banking activities which overlap or have an interaction with financial activities under the domain of other financial sector regulators.

Supervision and legislation on the functioning of banks and financial institutions is also done by the Ministry of Finance (under Central Government) through the Department of Financial Services. The Department of Financial Services does:

- Monitoring of banking operations
- Prescribes norms for the operation of public sector banks.
- Looks into the recovery of bank debts by way of examining legislative measures and establishing judicial mechanisms for the same.

Forms of Banks
There could be different form of banks as distinguished by the regulator:

State-owned banks

State Bank of India (SBI) is the largest state-owned bank and has been established under a special statute, the State Bank of India Act, 1955. Additionally, between the years

1969 to 1980, the government nationalized several banks by a legislative mandate.

Universal banks, commercial and retail banks

Universal banks are full-service banks and offer almost an entire range of financial products. They can be differentiated as private sector banks (non-state owned), public sector banks (state-owned) and foreign banks. As mentioned earlier licensing and operations of these banks fall under Banking Regulation Act.

Investment Banks

These banks give investment advisory and related services. Investment banks are governed by the Securities Exchange Board of India (SEBI). The license is also issued by SEBI.

Other Banks

For the purpose of providing banking services to underdeveloped and non-urban sectors, the banking sector has introduced special purpose banks – Cooperative Banks which cater to rural populace and small borrowers. They are formed on a co-operative basis and governed by cooperative laws formed by the state government and central banking laws. Additionally, regional rural banks were incorporated under the Regional Rural Banks Act, 1976 to develop the rural economy.

To promote financial inclusion, the Reserve Bank of India also introduced Payments Banks and Small Finance Banks. These offer basic and limited services like deposits, issuing payment instruments, savings vehicles and credit.

Banking License

Any entity that wants to do banking business has to obtain the license from the Reserve Bank of India (RBI). The license also entails the licensee to conduct ancillary business like guarantee and indemnity business, financial leasing, hire purchase business, securitization, trade finance besides borrowing and lending.

However, for dealing in foreign exchange, a separate license is required to be obtained under the Foreign Exchange Management Act.

Application Process for a banking license

Form for application of banking license is as per the Banking Regulation Rules, 1949. Different forms are applicable based on nature of applicant or whether it is a domestic or foreign company.

The application form for the license has to be submitted with the company's constitutional documents and balance sheet & profit & loss statements for last 5 years (for an existing company).

This is beside a host of information as mentioned in the form like information on ultimate individual promoters, information on various entities which are part of the promoter group, information on the persons/entities subscribing to or more than 5% of the paid-up equity capital, proposed management of the bank.

Also, a project report has to be submitted showing business potential, financial services proposed, plan for various compliances, plan for financial inclusion.

Corporate Governance

The Companies Act 2013, prescribes the corporate governance rules for banks in the country. However, for listed banking companies SEBI Regulations, 2015 are also applicable. SEBI regulations are primarily listing obligations and disclosures.

Banking Regulation Act, 1949

The Banking Regulation Act, 1949 is a legislation in India that regulates all banking firms in India.[1] Passed as the Banking Companies Act 1949, it came into force from 16 March 1949 and changed to Banking Regulation Act 1949 from 1 March 1966. It is applicable in jammu and Kashmir from 1956. Initially, the law was applicable only to banking companies. But, 1965 it was amended to make it applicable to cooperative banks and to introduce other changes.[2] In 2020 it was amended to bring the cooperative banks under the supervision of the Reserve Bank of India.

Overview

The Act provides a framework under which commercial banking in India is supervised and regulated. The Act supplements the Companies Act, 1956.[4] Primary Agricultural Credit Society and cooperative land mortgage banks are excluded from the Act.[2]

The Act gives the Reserve Bank of India (RBI) the power to license banks, have regulation over shareholding and voting rights of shareholders; supervise the appointment of the boards and management; regulate the operations of banks; lay down instructions for audits; control moratorium, mergers and liquidation; issue directives in the interests of public good and on banking policy, and impose penalties.[2]

In 1965, the Act was amended to include cooperative banks under its purview by adding the Section 56. Cooperative banks, which operate only in one state, are formed and run by the state government. But, RBI controls the licensing and regulates the business operations.[2] The Banking Act was a supplement to the previous acts related to banking.

Amendments

In 2020, Finance Minister Nirmala Sitaraman introduced a bill to amend the Act. The bill sought to bring all cooperative banks under the Reserve Bank of India. It brought bring 1,482 urban and 58 multi-state cooperative banks under the supervision of the RBI. The bill granted the RBI ability to reconstruct or merge banks without moratoriums. The bill was passed by the parliament.

Reserve Bank of India Act, 1934 Reserve Bank of India Act, 1934 is the legislative act under which the Reserve Bank of India was formed. This act along with the Companies Act, which was amended in 1936, were meant to provide a framework for the supervision of banking firms in India.

The Act contains the definition of the so-called scheduled banks, as they are mentioned in the 2nd Schedule of the Act. These are banks which were to have paid up capital and reserves above 5 lakh.

There are various section in the RBI Act but the most controversial and confusing section is Section 7. Although this section has been used only once by the central govt,[3] it puts a restriction on the autonomy of the RBI. **Section 7** states that central government can legislate the functioning of the RBI through the RBI board, and the RBI is not an autonomous body.

Section 17 of the Act defines the manner in which the RBI (the central bank of India) can conduct business. The RBI can accept deposits from the central and state governments without interest. It can purchase and discount bills of exchange from commercial banks. It can purchase foreign exchange from banks and sell it to them. It can provide loans to banks and state financial corporations. It can provide advances to the central government and state governments. It can buy or sell government securities. It can deal in derivative, repo and reverse repo.

Section 18 deals with emergency loans to banks. Section 21 states that the RBI must conduct banking affairs for the central government and manage public debt. Section 22 states that only the RBI has the exclusive rights to issue currency notes in India. Section 24 states that the maximum denomination a note can be is ?10,000 (US$130).

Section 26 of Act describes the legal tender character of Indian bank notes.

Section 28 allows the RBI to form rules regarding the exchange of damaged and imperfect notes.

Section 31 states that in India, only the RBI or the central government can issue and accept promissory notes that are payable on demand. However, cheques, that are payable on demand, can be issued by anyone.

Section 42(1) says that every scheduled bank must have an average daily balance with the RBI. The amount of the deposit shall be more that a certain percentage of its net time and demand liabilities in India.

BANKING SECTOR REFORM SINCE 1991

BANKING SECTOR REFORM SINCE 1991 Banking sector reforms were an important part of the broader agenda of structural economic reforms introduced in India in 1991. The first stage of reforms was shaped by the recommendations of the Committee on the Financial System (Narasimham Committee), which submitted its report in December 1991, suggesting reforms in banking, the government debt market, the stock markets, and in insurance, all aimed at producing a more efficient financial sector. Subsequently, the East Asian crisis in 1997 led to a heightened appreciation of the importance of a strong banking system, not just for efficient financial intermediation but also as an essential condition for macroeconomic stability. Recognizing this, the government appointed a Committee on Banking Sector Reforms to review the progress of reforms in banking and to consider further steps to strengthen the banking system in light of changes taking place in international financial markets and the experience of other developing countries. The two reports provided a road map that has guided the broad direction of reforms in this sector.

Pre-reform Situation

India's commercial banking system in 1991 had many of the problems typical of unreformed banking systems in many developing countries. There was extensive financial repression, reflected in detailed controls on interest rates, and large preemption of bank resources to finance the government deficit through the imposition of high statutory liquidity ratio (SLR), which prescribed investment in government securities at low interest rates. The system was also dominated by public sector banks, which accounted for 90 percent of total banking sector assets, reflecting the impact of two rounds of nationalization of private sector banks above a certain size, first in 1969 and again in 1983. These banks were nationalized because of the perception that it was necessary to impose social control over banking to give it a developmental thrust, with a special emphasis on extending banking in rural areas. The system suffered from inadequate prudential regulations, and nontransparent accounting practices. Supervision by the Reserve Bank of India (RBI) was also weak.

Broad Approach to Reform

The strategy for banking reforms was broadly similar to that followed in other countries, but with some important differences. It was similar to the extent that it focused on imposing prudential norms and improving regulatory supervision to meet Basel I standards (standards that were formulated by the committee of the Bank of International Settlement, or BIS, based in Basel, Switzerland), and it aimed at increasing competition to promote greater efficiency. However, there were two important differences compared with reforms in other countries. First, the reforms in banking were much more gradualist than in most countries, a course of action that was in line with the general strategy of reforms in India, made possible by the fact that the reforms were not introduced in the midst of a banking sector crisis, which might have entailed greater urgency. Second, unlike the case in many other countries, there was never any intention to privatize public sector banks. It was clearly recognized that competition was desirable, and this implied that both private sector banks and foreign banks should be allowed to expand their market share if they could. However, the government also declared its intention to strengthen public sector banks and enable them to meet competition.

There was also a great deal of progress in introducing prudential norms for income recognition, asset classification, and capital adequacy in a phased manner. As a consequence of this gradualist process, income recognition norms and capital adequacy norms have been fully aligned with Basel I standards, while asset recognition norms, though still falling short of international best practice, are now close to existing international standards.

Decontrol of Interest Rates and Credit

There has been a significant liberalization of interest rate and credit controls on commercial banks. Earlier, there were detailed restrictions on interest rates that could be paid on different types of deposits and rates that were charged to various categories of customers. These have been extensively liberalized. On the deposit side, interest rates paid on term deposits have been decontrolled, except that the RBI prescribes a maximum interest rate on short-term (15-day) deposits and also prescribes the interest rate on savings deposits. On the lending side, the detailed structure of interest rates prescribed for different types of borrowers and for different sizes of loans has been abolished; the RBI prescribes only the interest rate to be paid under the differential rate of interest scheme a very small window for loans to individuals below the poverty line. For the rest, individual banks fix lending rates with reference to the prime lending rate fixed by the bank. The reforms also abolished the requirement that banks needed to obtain RBI approval for individual credit limits fixed for large customers. With these changes, decisions on the cost of credit and the volume of credit to be extended have been left to bank management, subject to internal guidelines and procedures for credit approval and general prudential limits on single borrower and single project exposure.

Directed Credit

Reducing directed credit requirements is a common feature of banking reforms, and this was the case in India as well. A major directed credit requirement was constituted by the high levels of the SLR, which preempted bank resources to finance the government deficit at low interest rates. Preemption of credit by the government also occurred indirectly because the RBI followed a practice of automatically issuing ad hoc Treasury bills to meet any shortfalls in the government's balances with the RBI. Since this implied a mechanical transmission of fiscal expansion to the monetary side, it was offset by imposing a high cash reserve ratio (CRR) in the commercial banks, thus effectively crowding out private sector credit.

At one stage, prior to the reforms, the combined effect of the high CRR and the SLR was such that only 35 percent of the increment in bank deposits was actually available for commercial advances, the rest being either impounded by the RBI in the form of cash reserve deposits or absorbed by the government. The practice of automatic monetization was abandoned in 1994, and both the CRR and the SLR were reduced over time from 15 percent and 38.5 percent, respectively, before the reforms to 5 percent and 25 percent by 2005. The fiscal deficit is now financed through the auction of government securities conducted by the RBI, and in that sense, the interest rate on government borrowing is market-determined. However, it is interesting to note that, despite the reduction in the SLR from 38.5 percent to 25 percent, the proportion of government securities held by the banks to their total assets has actually increased from 30.4 percent at the end of March 1994 to 34.5 percent at the end of March 2004. This has occurred because of the combined effect of the inability to reduce the fiscal deficit—a key weakness of the reforms to date—and the fact that the prudential norms give sovereign debt a very low risk weight. In other words, while statutory preemption of bank resources was steadily reduced in the 1990s, the banks' appetite for government debt has remained high because the prudential norms contain a built-in regulatory bias in favor of government debt in preference to commercial credit.

The other major form of directed credit was the requirement that 40 percent of commercial credit has to be extended to the priority sector, which includes agriculture, small-scale industry, small transport operators, artisans, and so on. It applies to Indian commercial banks but not to foreign banks because the latter do not operate in rural areas and therefore cannot engage in agricultural lending. In their case, the requirement is that 15 percent of advances must be for exports and for the small-scale sector. These provisions have not been altered by the reforms. However, although the priority sector target for Indian banks has not been changed, the provision has been liberalized indirectly to some extent by definitional changes that expand the range of borrowers that are eligible. It is also worth noting that while banks are subject to sectoral direction of credit, they are not required to lend to particular borrowers; the credit decision of lending to a particular borrower is left to the bank on the basis of normal credit-worthiness analysis.

Banking Supervision

Improved prudential regulation must be supported by strong supervision, and several steps have been taken in this area since 1991. A Board of Financial Supervision, with an advisory council and an independent department of supervision, was established in the RBI. Traditional on-site supervision was supplemented by a system of offsite supervision, which allows a closer and more continuous monitoring of asset quality. A new supervisory reporting system was introduced in 1995, using the CAMELs approach (capital adequacy, asset quality, management, earnings, liquidity, and system for risk assessment) to assess the financial position of banks. More recently, the RBI has moved from the Basel I risk-based approach to a system of risk-based assessment for selected public sector banks.

In 2003 the RBI introduced a framework of prompt corrective action under which banks falling short of predetermined critical levels of capital adequacy, percentage of nonperforming assets (NPAs), and return on assets would automatically trigger some mandatory corrective action and possibly also further nonmandatory actions. Properly implemented, this should ensure that banks falling below a certain standard would be forced to correct their market share. An effective framework for corrective action is particularly important in the Indian context, where there are a number of weak public sector banks, and in which corrective action is the best way of preventing regulatory forbearance.

Increasing Competition

Increasing competition within the banking sector was an integral part of the reforms as a means of promoting efficiency in the sector, and important steps were taken in this direction. New banking licenses for Indian private sector banks, which had not been granted for many years before the reforms, were granted, and several new Indian private sector banks were established in the 1990s. While some have fared poorly, others have prospered. Some of the best Indian private sector banks have modernized their banking operations commendably and have developed electronic banking capability fully comparable with foreign banks. They have also expanded their market share. Foreign banks, which were earlier subjected to a very restrictive policy, were allowed more liberal expansion opportunities. New foreign banks were licensed to enter the market, and existing banks were allowed to expand branches more liberally.

These changes had an impact on the banking system. At the end of March 1991, 90 percent of the assets of the banking system were accounted for by public sector banks, with the private Indian banks accounting for 3.7 percent and foreign banks 6.3 percent. By the end of March 2003, this had changed to 75 percent, 18.5 percent, and 6.9 percent, respectively. The major expansion in market share has been on the part of Indian private sector banks, though the extent of the increase is exaggerated because they include the effect of the merger of a major nongovernment development financing institution (ICICI) with its banking subsidiary to create a new bank, leading to the inclusion of its assets in the total for private bank assets.

The share of foreign banks has increased only marginally, despite a more liberal policy of branch expansion of this sector. This reflects the fact that these banks are focused primarily on high-end corporate clients, who are in any case moving away from bank financing, relying increasingly upon the capital markets to raise finance. The income-earning strategy of foreign banks is correspondingly oriented toward greater reliance upon feebased income.

Public Sector Banks

Unlike banking reforms in most developing countries, India's banking sector reforms abjured privatization; the strategy from the very outset was that public sector banks would remain publicly owned but would be made to improve their performance by a combination of better supervision and greater managerial autonomy.

While ruling out privatization, public sector banks were encouraged to raise capital from the market, which diluted government equity, a dilution that was allowed as long as the government share remained 51 percent. The induction of private shareholders was expected to help the banks meet capital adequacy requirements without putting a strain on the budget. It was also expected to create a more commercial environment and thereby also to condition the attitude of government, even though the government remained a majority shareholder. Twenty of the public sector banks were able to raise capital from the market, and by 2005 the private shareholding in these banks varied from 20 percent to 46 percent.

A number of steps were taken to improve the efficiency of public sector banks, including rationalizing the branch network and reducing the labor force through voluntary retirement plans. Productivity enhancement through information technology application was also pursued, though public sector banks were slower than others in introducing electronic banking. However, some of the better public sector banks now offer online banking facilities at a large number of their branches. The fact that public sector banks have to observe the public sector salary structure remains an important limitation, and this is likely to become more of a constraint as the size of the private banking sector expands. However, within this constraint, public sector banks have made efforts to improve recruitment and develop better human resource development policies

Skeptics remain unconvinced that public sector banks can ever be managed in a way that distances government from individual banking decisions. The problem in India is not so much political intervention in individual credit decisions as the imposition of procedures that make it difficult for bank managers to take initiative in making commercial decisions without being accused of having extended undue favors. This is primarily because the law equates the employees of any entity in which the government has a 51 percent stake with civil servants, making them subject to the same standards of accountability for their actions. This places a great deal of emphasis on compliance with procedures, which forces bank management to be cautious and rule-bound rather than innovative.

Despite these constraints, the evidence suggests that public sector banks have improved their performance in the postreform period. Gross nonperforming loans of public sector banks declined from 17.8 percent at the end of March 1997 to 9.4 percent at the end of March 2003. Net nonperforming loans as a percentage of total assets declined from 3.6 percent to 1.9 percent over the same period. Net profit in public sector banks as a percentage of total assets increased from 0.6 percent in 1996–1997 to 1.0 percent in 2002–2003, and operating expenses as a percentage of total assets declined from 2.9 percent to 2.3 percent in the same period.

Banking System Performance

The impact of the reforms on the efficiency of the banking system in performing its twin roles of financial intermediation and resource allocation is not easy to evaluate. As far as the scale of bank intermediation is concerned, the ratio of total credit extended by the banking system to India's gross domestic product has increased, but it is still relatively low compared to countries such as China or some of the other East Asian countries. The ratio in India increased from 51.5 percent in 1990 to 53.4 percent in 2000, whereas in China it increased from 90 percent to 132.7 percent in the same period. The figures over the same period are also much higher for Malaysia (75.7% and 143.4%) and Thailand (91.1% and 121.7%), though many Latin American countries have figures closer to those of India.

There is evidence of significant improvement in several dimensions in recent years. Gross nonperforming assets (NPAs) as a percentage of total advances have fallen from 15.7 percent in 1996–1997 to 7.3 percent in 2003–2004. Gross NPAs as a percent of total assets are much lower because Indian banks typically have a large proportion of their assets in sovereign debt; this ratio has also declined from 7 percent in 1996–1997 to 4 percent in 2002–2003. More importantly, the financial strength of the banks is actually better than it appears from these ratios because Indian banks do not write off assets, even though large provisions have been made. Net nonperforming assets, calculated after taking account of provisioning, are 3 percent of total advances and only around 2 percent of total assets. There has been a general improvement in other financial indicators, such as net profit as a percentage of total assets, interest spread as a percentage of assets, and operating expenses as a percentage of total assets, for public sector banks, old private sector banks, new private sector banks, and foreign banks. The financial strength of the banks, as measured by the capital to risk adjusted assets ratio (CRAR), shows distinct improvement in the postreform period. The required CRAR was increased in phases, to 8 percent at first (which is the Basel I minimum) and then to 9 percent in 1999–2000. Initially, banks with insufficient capital had to be capitalized by the injection of government equity from the budget, but subsequently several banks were able to raise capital from the market, and this, combined with plowing back of profits, led to a substantial improvement in capital adequacy. At the end of March 2003, out of the 93 commercial banks operating in India, 91 were above 9 percent and as many as 87 were above 10 percent, compared with only 54 out of 92 banks above 9 percent and 42 above 10 percent at the end of March 1996. It is noteworthy that the Indian banking system did not suffer from any contagion effect in the aftermath of the East Asian crisis. However, this is not so much due to the improvements brought about after 1991, as the fact that the capital account was not fully open. Banks were not allowed to undertake excessive foreign currency exposure, and external borrowing (especially short-term borrowing) was strictly controlled. This cautious policy helped insulate India from the severe reversals of external flows witnessed in many emerging market countries in the 1990s.

The Future Agenda

The agenda for banking reforms in the future involves the continuation of the process of aligning prudential norms and supervision systems to the best international practices. This is bound to be a moving target since the banking system internationally is shifting from Basel I to Basel II (standards formulated by the committee of the Bank of International Settlement, or BIS, based in Basel,

Switzerland), which involves use of much more sophisticated and bank-specific methods of risk assessment. An immediate challenge facing the public sector banks relates to the case for merging some of the banks to create stronger banks with a larger capital base and therefore correspondingly larger capacity to finance large projects. Given the size of the economy and its projected growth, there is a case for having at least two banks at a scale comparable to the larger Asian banks.

A general problem affecting the banking system (both public sector and private sector banks) is the efficacy of the legal system in enforcing creditor rights. At present the legal procedure is dilatory, and there are difficulties associated with enforcing recovery through seizure and sale of collateral or through forced liquidation. Recent changes in the law enable banks to seize collateral, but the process of the sale of collateral remains difficult. Legislation was introduced in 2003, though not yet enacted, to make it easier to force liquidation in cases where bank debts are overdue and no agreement is reached between the creditor and the borrower on restructuring the debt. There is also a need for a credit information bureau that would enable banks to access information on the credit standing of prospective borrowers based on their status with other banks. The Credit Information Bureau of India was set up for this purpose in 2000, and the government has announced that it will introduce legislation to enable the bureau to obtain information from participatory banks with suitable safeguards protecting privacy. Improvements in the legal environment for recovery of bank dues and institutionalization of information sharing among banks will make a major contribution to increasing the efficiency of bank intermediation.